DIABETIC MEAL PREP FOR BEGINNERS

Diabetic Cookbook with 30-Day Meal Plan to Prevent and Reverse Diabetes

AMZ PUBLISHING

TABLE OF CONTENTS

67

INTRODUCTION

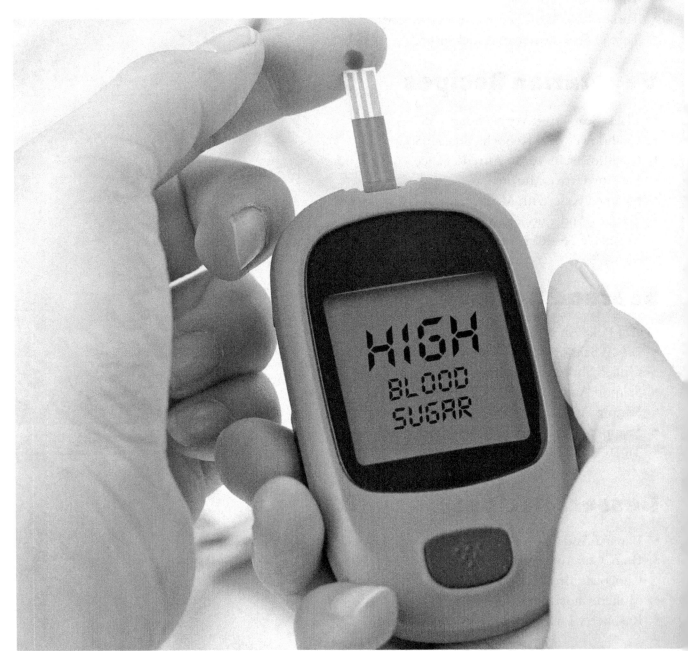

WHAT IS DIABETES?

Diabetes is one of the most common issues affecting the general US population.

As per the figures in the Centers for Disease Control and Prevention (CDC), an estimated 1.4 million cases of diabetes are diagnosed each year in the United States of America.

Not only this, the issue runs deeper, as there are an estimated 8.1 million people who are believed to be unwittingly living with the disease.

This means that 9.4 percent of the general US population is suffering from diabetes.

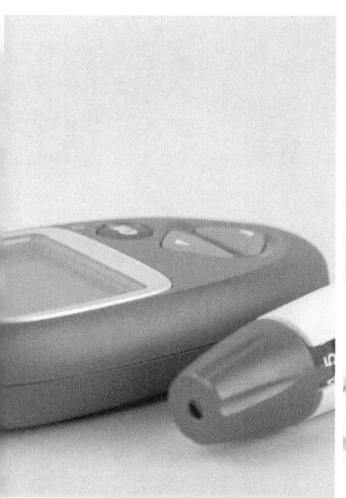

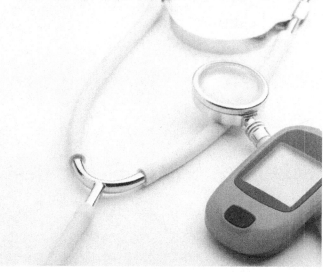

Primarily, diabetes is of three types. The majority of diabetes patients have type 2 diabetes, which is preventable through medication and diet.

Diabetes is a disease that is the result of high blood glucose in the human body. In a diabetic patient, the insulin that helps transform glucose into energy does not always produce enough insulin.

This prevents glucose from reaching the cells, resulting in diabetes. Though diabetes is not curable, if the disease is left untreated, it can cause various bodily complications.

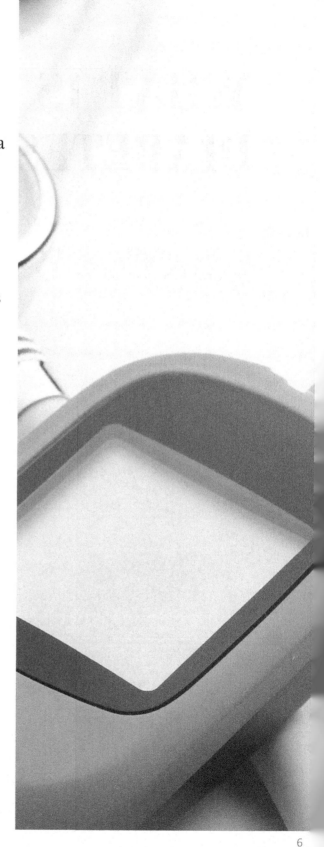

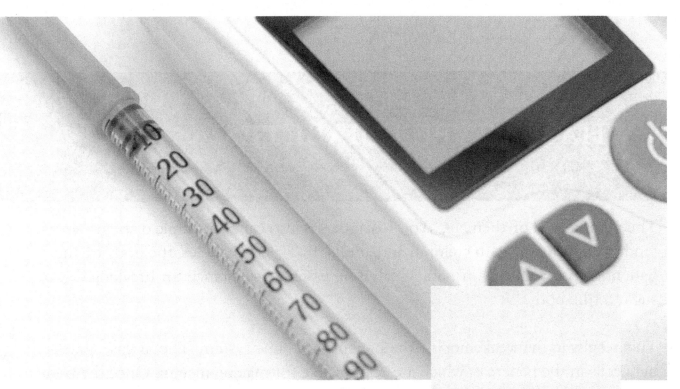

TYPES OF DIABETES

The three most common kinds of diabetes are

1. **Type 1 diabetes** (pancreas's failure to produce enough insulin)
2. **Type 2 diabetes** (cells' failure to respond to insulin)
3. **Gestational diabetes** (pregnant women with a history of diabetes develop high blood sugar levels).

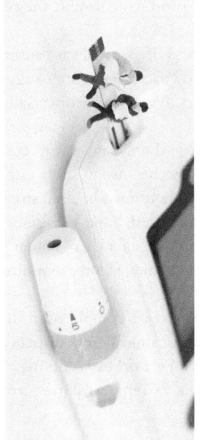

WHAT IS TYPE 1 DIABETES?

The most feared of them all, Type 1 diabetes is also called 'juvenile diabetes,' as it tends to develop in both children and adults. In Type 1 diabetes, the body of the patient stops producing insulin, which is an essential substance for breaking down sugar in the body.

This results in the weakening of the patient's immune system. The disease attacks the beta cells in the pancreas, which are responsible for making insulin. Once the body stops producing insulin, the patient with Type 1 diabetes must take insulin every day.

The loss of beta cells is caused by the autoimmune response, whose source is still unknown. Some theories suggest that Type 1 diabetes may be influenced by genetic factors. A family member with a similar condition may be a carrier of the risk.

Because there is no way to cure the disease, a patient suffering from Type 1 diabetes must receive insulin shots just under the skin or receive insulin via an insulin pump. The patient must be on a strict diet and exercise regime throughout their life. When left untreated, Type 1 diabetes can cause complications such as diabetic ketoacidosis and nonketotic hyperosmolar coma. Long-term complications include heart disease, stroke, kidney failure, foot ulcers, and eye damage.

Furthermore, complications may arise from low blood sugar caused by excessive insulin dosing. Type 1 diabetes accounts for an estimated 5–10% of all diabetes cases across the world. Symptoms of Type 1 diabetes include increased thirst, increased hunger, extreme weakness, irritability, abdominal pain, foot ulcers, and weak eyesight.

WHAT IS TYPE 2 DIABETES?

This is the most common type of diabetes found today. Type 2 diabetes is very prevalent among both young and old. One of the main reasons for this is the nature of our lifestyles and our lack of physical exercise. The disease occurs due to obesity and a lack of exercise.

People with a genetic history of the disease are also vulnerable to acquiring Type 2 diabetes. While once found in people over 35 years of age, Type 2 diabetes is today found in youth as well. At least 90 percent of diabetic patients are found to be carrying traits of Type 2 diabetes.

This is a non-insulin type of disease, which means that although the patient has high blood sugar, they don't need to take insulin shots regularly. The bodies of patients with Type 2 diabetes produce insulin but not enough to break down glucose.

The prevention of Type 2 diabetes includes checking one's weight, getting regular physical exercise, and following a healthy diet and lifestyle. This should be enough to regulate the smooth flow of blood sugar levels. If the patient still cannot control their diabetes, medication is usually prescribed by a doctor.

The symptoms of Type 2 diabetes are not as noticeable as those for Type 1 diabetes. However, one should always be careful to not put on extra weight or give up on physical exercise.

WHAT IS GESTATIONAL DIABETES?

This type of diabetes develops in women, mostly during or just after pregnancy. In gestational diabetes, the woman can develop high blood sugar levels. Pregnant women without any prior history of high blood sugar/diabetes are also found to develop gestational diabetes.

The disease seems to vanish after the child is born. Also, in some cases, after the child is born, the mother develops the signs and symptoms of Type 2 diabetes. Women who develop gestational diabetes during their pregnancies are believed to have a higher probability of developing Type 2 diabetes in the later stages of life. It is hard to identify the symptoms of gestational diabetes. The disease increases the possibility of pre-eclampsia, depression, and cesarean section delivery.

A mother should receive proper medical treatment during her pregnancy. Mothers who have a history of any illness tend to develop a risk regarding the delivery of a normal child. In certain cases, the child may be prone to low blood sugar after birth, or to jaundice. Children can also face a greater risk of developing Type 2 diabetes in the later stages of their lives.

A patient suffering from gestational diabetes should observe a healthy lifestyle and food habits.

An Appeal from the Publisher

Hello wonderful reader!

We hope you are enjoying this book.

We wanted to let you know that you have made an impact on many lives by purchasing this book.

Just to give you a brief introduction: We are a small publishing company with a team of 8 writers and 2 editors.

Most of our employees come from financially weaker section and our company is the only means they support their families. This is our way of giving back to the society.

We don't have the giant advertising budgets that many other publishers and businesses do online.

So, one way that you can really support our mission and our business is by leaving us a review on this book.

For a small company like us, getting reviews (especially on Amazon) means we can submit our books for advertising.

This means we can actually sell a few copies from time to time and make a bigger impact on the society as a whole. So, every review means a lot to us.

We can't THANK YOU enough for this!

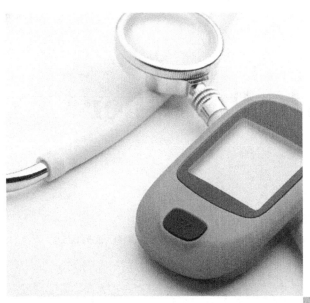

HOW CAN DIABETES BE PREVENTED AND CONTROLLED?

One of the best ways to prevent or control diabetes is to change your lifestyle and food habits.

Once an ailment found predominantly in people over 35 years old, diabetes is creeping into our lives and affecting the health of young people. Obesity and a lack of physical exercise are the prime causes of diabetes.

Patients with Type 1 diabetes need to rely on insulin, either injected or provided through a pump, to maintain the insulin level in their bodies.

In addition, a diet, usually prescribed by a doctor, should be strictly followed to counter the damage done by Type 1 diabetes.

Strokes: Diabetes also attacks the heart by damaging the blood vessels, which could lead to various heart-related diseases and cause stroke. The patient should maintain a permissible blood sugar level at all times and quit smoking.

Hypoglycemia is a condition involving low blood glucose levels. Diabetic patients suffering from low blood glucose levels should consult a doctor for medicine and should also follow a strict diet plan.

Other diseases that might affect a diabetic patient are chronic kidney disease, foot ulcers, damaged nerves, and weakened eyesight.

Preventing diabetes requires lifestyle management, which is the best remedy for a diabetes patient.

FOODS TO EAT AND FOODS TO AVOID

The prime objective of any food plan for a diabetic patient is to control their blood sugar level. Here is a list of foods that the patient should opt for and avoid to control diabetes:

FOODS TO EAT:

- Fatty fish: a great source of omega-3 fatty acids. Reduces inflammation and good for fighting heart ailments.
- Leafy green vegetables: a rich source of vitamin C and essential nutrients. Improves the eyesight.
- Cinnamon: improves insulin sensitivity, cholesterol.

- Eggs, poultry products: increases HDL cholesterol level.

-

- Chia seeds: high in fiber content, helps in controlling weight.

- Turmeric: reduces inflation, keeps blood sugar levels in check, and prevents heart disease.

- Greek yogurt: maintains a healthy blood sugar level and prevents heart disease.

- Nuts: high in fiber and provides essential digestible carbohydrates. Helps regulate the insulin level.

- Broccoli: low-calorie, low in carbs.

- Extra-virgin olive oil: contains monounsaturated fat that is healthy for the heart.

- Flax seeds: help reduce inflammation and control the blood sugar level.

- Apple cider vinegar: improves insulin sensitivity in a diabetic patient and lowers blood sugar levels

- Strawberries: anti-inflammatory in nature.

- Garlic: lowers the LDL cholesterol level, lower inflation, and keeps the blood sugar level in check.

- Whole grains: contain high fiber content and are low on the glycemic index scale.

- Beans: rich in protein and low on the GI scale.

- Sweet potatoes: great source of vitamins A and C, potassium, and fiber.

FOOD TO AVOID:

- Melons and pineapple: have a high GI level.
- Carbohydrate-rich food: any food item that is high in carbs should be avoided by patients suffering from diabetes.
- Saturated fats/Trans-fats: heavily processed foods such as fries and chips should be avoided.
- Refined sugar/Sugar-infused drinks: soda, energy drinks, shakes that are high in sugar.
- Salty food: foods high in salt content can raise the blood sugar level in the body.
- Alcohol/tobacco: moderate use only. Patients on an induced insulin prescription should avoid them.

- White bread/Rice: high carbohydrate content and low in fiber.
- Honey, maple Syrup: causes the blood sugar level to increase.
- Packaged foods: highly processed

The diet of a diabetic patient should be rich in vegetables, fruits, nuts, and proteins. The trick is not to avoid food but, rather, to consume the right balance of certain foods.

WHY MEAL PREP?

With life always on the move, most of us find it hard to make food every day. This often causes us to opt out of the kitchen and get ready-to-cook or outside food that is highly processed and full of ingredients waiting to shoot up the blood sugar levels that we are trying so hard to control. Therefore, this book contains recipes that can be made in advance and stored for later consumption. This is called meal prepping.

With the help of the detailed instructions, you can easily stay on the 30-day meal plan. The recipes are easy to prepare and can be your plus-one even if you plan to visit friends or family at the end of a busy weekend. Prepping meals helps you ditch the nearest drive-thru offering full of carbs and sugar. Prepping also helps you save money.

Every recipe in this book indicates the exact amount of ingredients one needs to prepare the meal. Therefore, by making an easy calculation, you can determine how much money you will need when prepping your meals.

COMMON MISTAKES TO AVOID WHILE MEAL PREPPING

STOCKING OF FOOD: This is the most common mistake a beginner can make. Prepping food in advance should not be confused with preparing in bulk. Be aware of how much food can be stored for later use.

Because food has a maturity cycle, keeping food in bulk will only lead you to overstuff your refrigerator and end up eating stale food.

WASTAGE OF FOOD: Read your meal plan very carefully and try not to indulge in an extended shopping spree. Many people tend to buy in bulk while prepping food.

LAST-MINUTE SHOPPING: Always find time to buy ingredients for your meal well in advance. Last-minute shopping often leads you to miss important details.

BEING IN A RUSH: Whenever you are preparing food, ensure that you have enough time to do so. If you're in a rush, you may miss important instructions.

USING STOCKED ITEMS: Try to use fresh food while meal prepping. You will likely be storing the recipes that you make, so using fresh food will boost the meals' nutritional value.

30-Days Meal Plan

Day	Breakfast	Lunch	Dinner
1	Healthy Cottage Cheese Pancakes	Beef and Zucchini Lasagna	Tomato and Zucchini Sauté + Raspberry Pumpkin Muffin
2	Avocado Lemon Toast	Turkey and Avocado Patties	Steamed Kale with Mediterranean Dressing
3	Healthy Baked Eggs	Easy and Healthy Beef Fajitas	Vegetable Noodles Stir-Fry + Raspberry Pumpkin Muffin
4	Quick Low-Carb Oatmeal	Baked Salmon Served with Garlic Butter	Tuscan-Style Rosemary Chicken
5	Tofu and Vegetable Scramble	Broccoli and Marinated Steak	Black Bean and Veggie Soup Topped with Lime Salsa
6	Breakfast Smoothie Bowl with Fresh Berries	Salmon and Shredded Potato Patties	Grilled Shrimps with Yogurt and Chili Sauce
7	Chia and Coconut Pudding	Lemon-Flavored Chicken Piccata	Chicken and Veggie Stew + Bran, Oat, and Banana Cookies
8	Avocado Lemon Toast	Turkey Rolls with Pecans and Cranberry	Snapper Fillets with Parsley Celery Salad and Tahini Dressing
9	Breakfast Smoothie Bowl with Fresh Berries	Chicken and Cauliflower Casserole	Tuna and Avocado Salad
10	Quick Low-Carb Oatmeal	Shrimp and Jalapeno Veggie Bake	Cauliflower in Vegan Alfredo Sauce
11	Chia and Coconut Pudding	Roasted Veggies with Flank Steak	Healthy Carrot Muffins + Raspberry Pumpkin Muffin
12	Healthy Cottage Cheese Pancakes	Beef and Zucchini Lasagna	Quick Bison Meatballs
13	Healthy Baked Eggs	Baked Salmon Served with Garlic Butter	Vegetable Noodles Stir-Fry + Chocolate Brownies
14	Breakfast Smoothie Bowl with Fresh Berries	Easy and Healthy Beef Fajitas	Tomato and Zucchini Sauté
15	Quick Low-Carb Oatmeal	Broccoli and Marinated Steak	Snapper Fillets with Parsley Celery Salad and Tahini Dressing
16	Healthy Cottage Cheese Pancakes	Turkey and Avocado Patties	Steamed Kale with Mediterranean Dressing + Banana and Chocolate Mug Cake
17	Chia and Coconut Pudding	Chicken and Cauliflower Casserole	Black Bean and Veggie Soup Topped with Lime Salsa
18	Avocado Lemon Toast	Beef and Zucchini Lasagna	Grilled Shrimps with Yogurt and Chili Sauce
19	Healthy Baked Eggs	Baked Salmon Served with Garlic Butter	Tuscan-Style Rosemary Chicken + Bran, Oat, and Banana Cookies
20	Healthy Cottage Cheese Pancakes	Lemon-Flavored Chicken Piccata	Vegetable Noodles Stir-Fry
21	Breakfast Smoothie Bowl with Fresh Berries	Salmon and Shredded Potato Patties	Snapper Fillets with Parsley Celery Salad and Tahini Dressing
22	Healthy Baked Eggs	Turkey Rolls with Pecans and Cranberry	Black Bean and Veggie Soup Topped with Lime Salsa
23	Quick Low-Carb Oatmeal	Shrimp and Jalapeno Veggie Bake	Tuna and Avocado Salad
24	Healthy Cottage Cheese Pancakes	Lemon-Flavored Chicken Piccata	Steamed Kale with Mediterranean Dressing + Molten Chocolate Cake
25	Chia and Coconut Pudding	Quick Bison Meatballs	Tuscan-Style Rosemary Chicken
26	Avocado Lemon Toast	Chicken and Cauliflower Casserole	Grilled Shrimps with Yogurt and Chili Sauce + Chocolate Brownies
27	Quick Low-Carb Oatmeal	Broccoli and Marinated Steak	Cauliflower in Vegan Alfredo Sauce
28	Healthy Baked Eggs	Baked Salmon Served with Garlic Butter	Black Beans and Veggie Soup Topped with Lime Salsa + Bran, Oat, and Banana Cookies
29	Breakfast Smoothie Bowl with Fresh Berries	Easy and Healthy Beef Fajitas	Steamed Kale with Mediterranean Dressing
30	Chia and Coconut Pudding	Turkey and Avocado Patties	Tomato and Zucchini Sauté + Banana and Chocolate Mug Cake

breakfast

RECIPES

AVOCADO LEMON TOAST

GENERAL INFO

Serving Size: 1
Servings per Recipe: 2
Calories: 72 calories per serving
Total Time: 13 minutes

NUTRITION INFO

Fat – 1.2 g
Protein – 3.6 g
Carbohydrates – 11.6 g

INGREDIENTS

Whole-grain bread – 2 slices
Avocado – 1/2
Fresh cilantro (chopped) – 2 tablespoons
Fresh lemon juice – 1 teaspoon
Lemon zest – ¼ teaspoon
Cayenne pepper – 1 pinch
Fine sea salt – 1 pinch
Chia seeds – ¼ teaspoon

DIRECTIONS

1. Start by taking a medium-sized mixing bowl and adding in the avocado. Use a fork to mash it nicely.
2. Add in the cilantro, lemon zest, lemon juice, sea salt, and cayenne pepper. Mix well until combined.
3. Toast the bread slices in a toaster until golden brown. This should take about 3 minutes.
4. Top the toasted bread slices with the avocado mixture and finish by sprinkling with chia seeds.

5. Storage Tip: You can prepare the avocado mixture and store it in the refrigerator for a day. To retain the freshness, make sure to use an airtight container.

BREAKFAST SMOOTHIE BOWL WITH FRESH BERRIES

GENERAL INFO

Serving Size: 1
Servings per Recipe: 2
Calories: 166 calories per serving
Total Time: 5 minutes

NUTRITION INFO

Fat – 9.2 g
Protein – 17.6 g
Carbohydrates – 4.1 g

INGREDIENTS

Almond milk (unsweetened) – ½ cup
Strawberries (chopped) – 2 ounces
Crushed ice – 3 cups
Pea protein powder – 1/3 cup
Psyllium husk powder – 1/2 teaspoon
Coconut oil – 1 tablespoon
Liquid stevia – 5 to 10 drops

DIRECTIONS

1. Start by taking a blender and adding in the crushed ice cubes. Let them sit for about 30 seconds.
2. Now add in the almond milk, chopped strawberries, pea protein powder, psyllium husk powder, coconut oil, and liquid stevia. Blend well until it turns into a smooth and creamy puree.
3. Empty the prepared smoothie into 2 glasses.
4. Top with coconut flakes and fresh strawberries.

Storage Tip: This smoothie can be transferred into an airtight container and stored in the freezer. Before serving, you can take out the frozen smoothie and let it rest for 5 minutes. Blend well and it is ready to serve!

CHIA AND COCONUT PUDDING

GENERAL INFO

Serving Size: 1
Servings per Recipe: 2
Calories: 201 calories per serving
Total Time: 5 minutes

NUTRITION INFO

Fat – 10 g
Protein – 5.4 g
Carbohydrates – 22.8 g

INGREDIENTS

Light coconut milk – 7 ounces
Chia seeds – ¼ cup
Liquid stevia – 3 to 4 drops
Clementine – 1
Kiwi – 1
Shredded coconut (unsweetened)

DIRECTIONS

1. Start by taking a mixing bowl and adding in the light coconut milk. Add in the liquid stevia to sweeten the milk. Mix well.
2. Add the chia seeds to the milk and whisk until well-combined. Set aside.
3. Peel the clementine and carefully remove the skin from the wedges. Set aside.
4. Also, peel the kiwi and dice it into small pieces.
5. Take a glass jar and assemble the pudding. For this, place the fruits at the bottom of the jar; then add a dollop of chia pudding. Now spread the fruits and then add another layer of chia pudding.
6. Finish by garnishing with the remaining fruits and shredded coconut.

Storage Tip: This can be stored in a glass jar in the fridge for a couple of days.

HEALTHY BAKED EGGS

GENERAL INFO

Serving Size: 1
Servings per Recipe: 6
Calories: 323 calories per serving
Total Time: 1 hour

INGREDIENTS

Olive oil – 1 tablespoon
Onion (chopped) – 1 medium
Garlic – 2 cloves
Spinach leaves – 8 ounces
Eggs – 8 large
Half-and-half – 1 cup
Sea salt – ½ teaspoon
Black pepper – 1 teaspoon
Shredded mozzarella cheese
(medium-fat) – 3 cups
Feta cheese – ½ cup
Olive oil spray

NUTRITION INFO

Fat – 22.3 g
Protein – 22.6 g
Carbohydrates – 7.9 g

HEALTHY BAKED EGGS

DIRECTIONS

1. Start by preheating the oven to 375°F.
2. Take a glass baking dish and grease it with olive oil spray. Set aside.
3. Now take a nonstick pan and pour in the olive oil. Place the pan on a medium flame and let it heat.
4. Once done, toss in the garlic, spinach, and onion. Cook for about 5 minutes. Set aside.
5. Now take a large mixing bowl and add in the half-and-half, eggs, pepper, and salt. Whisk well to combine.
6. Add in the feta cheese and shredded mozzarella cheese (reserve ½ cup of mozzarella cheese for later).
7. Add the egg mixture and prepared spinach to the prepared glass baking dish. Mix well to combine. Sprinkle the reserved cheese on top.
8. Bake the egg mix for about 45 minutes.
9. Remove the baking dish from the oven and let it stand for 10 minutes.
10. Slice and serve!

Storage Tip: You can increase the amount of ingredients and bake the egg in advance. This can be stored in the refrigerator for about 4 days. (Make sure to use a food-grade airtight container to store the eggs.) The eggs can be popped in the oven or microwave before eating.

HEALTHY COTTAGE CHEESE PANCAKES

HealthyRecipesBlog.com

GENERAL INFO

Serving Size: 2
Servings per Recipe: 1
Calories: 205 calories per serving
Total Time: 15

NUTRITION INFO

Fat – 1.5 g
Protein – 24.5 g
Carbohydrates – 19 g

INGREDIENTS

Cottage cheese (low-fat) – ½ cup
Oats – ¼ cup
Egg whites – ⅓ cup (approx. 2 egg whites)
Vanilla extract – 1 teaspoon
Stevia (raw) – 1 tablespoon
Olive oil cooking spray
Berries or sugar-free jam (optional)

DIRECTIONS

1. Start by taking a food blender and adding in the egg whites and cottage cheese. Also add in the vanilla extract, a little bit of stevia, and oats. Pulse until the consistency is smooth.
2. Take a nonstick pan and grease it nicely with the cooking spray. Place the pan on a medium flame.
3. Once heated, scoop out half of the batter and pour it on the pan. Cook for about 2½ minutes on each side.
4. Place the cooked pancakes on a serving plate and top with sugar-free jam or berries.

Storage Tip: Pancakes can be stored in the refrigerator in a food-grade zip-lock bag or airtight container for up to 4-5 days. The pancakes can be reheated in a nonstick pan before serving.

QUICK LOW-CARB OATMEAL

GENERAL INFO

Serving Size: 1
Servings per Recipe: 2
Calories: calories per serving
Total Time: 15 minutes

NUTRITION INFO

Fat – 24.3 g
Protein – 11.7 g
Carbohydrates – 16.7 g

INGREDIENTS

Almond flour – ½ cup
Coconut flour – 4 tablespoons
Flax meal – 2 tablespoons
Chia seeds – 2 tablespoons
Cinnamon (ground) – 1 teaspoon
Liquid stevia – 10 – 15 drops
Almond milk (unsweetened) – 1½ cups
Vanilla extract – 1 teaspoon
Salt – as per taste

DIRECTIONS

1. Start by taking a large mixing bowl and adding in the coconut flour, almond flour, ground cinnamon, flax seed powder, and chia seeds. Mix well to combine.
2. Place a stockpot on a medium flame and add in the dry ingredients. Also add in the liquid stevia, vanilla extract, and almond milk. Stir well to combine.
3. Cook the flour and almond milk for about 4 minutes. Add salt if required.
4. Transfer the oatmeal to a serving bowl and top with nuts, seeds, and fresh berries.

Storage Tip: The oatmeal can be transferred to an airtight container and stored in the refrigerator for about 3 days.

TOFU AND VEGETABLE SCRAMBLE

GENERAL INFO

Serving Size: 1
Servings per Recipe: 2
Calories: 238 calories per serving
Total Time: 15 minutes

INGREDIENTS

Firm tofu (drained) – 16 ounces
Tomato – 1 medium
Green bell pepper – 1 medium
Red onion – ½ medium
Sea salt – ½ teaspoon
Turmeric – ½ teaspoon
Garlic powder – 1 teaspoon
Cumin powder – 1 teaspoon
Chili powder – ¼ teaspoon
Water – 1 tablespoon
Fresh coriander – for garnishing
Lemon juice – for topping

NUTRITION INFO

Fat – 11 g
Protein – 20.5 g
Carbohydrates – 16.6 g

TOFU AND VEGETABLE SCRAMBLE

DIRECTIONS

1. Start by preparing the ingredients. For this, you need to remove the seeds of the tomato and green bell pepper. Chop the onion, bell pepper, and tomato into small cubes.
2. Take a small mixing bowl and place the firm tofu inside it. Use your hands to crumble the firm tofu. Set aside.
3. Take a nonstick pan and add in the onion, tomato, and bell pepper. Stir and cook for about 3 minutes.
4. Add the firm crumbled tofu to the pan and mix well.
5. Take a small bowl and add in the water, turmeric, garlic powder, cumin powder, and chili powder. Mix well and pour it over the tofu and vegetable mixture.
6. Let the tofu and vegetable crumble cook with spices for 5 minutes. Keep stirring so that the ingredients don't stick to the pan.
7. Sprinkle the tofu scramble with chili flakes and salt. Mix well.
8. Transfer the prepared scramble to a serving bowl and give it a nice drizzle of lemon juice.
9. Finish by garnishing with fresh coriander. Serve hot!

Storage Tip: Store the scramble in an airtight container in the refrigerator for up to 3 days.

An Appeal from the Publisher

Hello wonderful reader!

We hope you are enjoying this book.

We wanted to let you know that you have made an impact on many lives by purchasing this book.

Just to give you a brief introduction: We are a small publishing company with a team of 8 writers and 2 editors.

Most of our employees come from financially weaker section and our company is the only means they support their families. This is our way of giving back to the society.

We don't have the giant advertising budgets that many other publishers and businesses do online.

So, one way that you can really support our mission and our business is by leaving us a review on this book.

For a small company like us, getting reviews (especially on Amazon) means we can submit our books for advertising.

This means we can actually sell a few copies from time to time and make a bigger impact on the society as a whole. So, every review means a lot to us.

We can't THANK YOU enough for this!

meat

RECIPES

BEEF AND ZUCCHINI LASAGNA

GENERAL INFO

Serving Size: 1
Servings per Recipe: 4
Calories: 244 calories per serving
Total Time: 1 hour 30 minutes

NUTRITION INFO

Fat – 7.9 g
Protein – 30.4 g
Carbohydrates – 12.3 g

INGREDIENTS

Ground beef, 92% – 16 ounces
Zucchini – 2 medium
Onion – 4½ ounces
Garlic – 2 cloves
Serrano chili – 1
Tomatoes (skinned) – 3
Mushrooms – 5½ ounces
Chicken bouillon – ½ cube
Low-fat mozzarella (shredded) – ½ cup
Paprika – 1 teaspoon
Dried thyme – 1 teaspoon
Dried basil – 1 teaspoon
Salt – as per taste
Pepper – as per taste
Cooking spray

BEEF AND ZUCCHINI LASAGNA

DIRECTIONS

1. Start by making ½-inch slices of zucchini using a julienne peeler.
2. Once done, sprinkle all the zucchini slices with salt. Set aside for about 10 minutes.
3. Use a paper towel to blot excess water from the zucchini slices. Place them on a baking sheet.
4. Place the baking sheet in the oven and broil for about 3 minutes. Make sure that the heat setting is on high.
5. Once done, place the broiled zucchini slices on kitchen paper towels.
6. Chop the onions, chili, garlic, mushrooms, and skinned tomatoes roughly. Set them aside.
7. Take a deep nonstick skillet and grease it using cooking spray. Place it over a medium-high flame.
8. Now add the onion, garlic, and chili to the heated skillet and cook for about 1 minute.
9. Toss in the mushrooms and tomatoes. Sauté the veggies for another 4 minutes. Turn off the heat and empty the ingredients into a bowl.
10. Place the same skillet over a medium flame and add in the ground beef. Sprinkle with paprika and cook until the meat turns brown.
11. Return the cooked vegetables to the pan and mix well. Also add in the chicken bouillon, paprika, dried thyme, and dried basil. Mix well and cook for about 25 minutes over a low flame.

BEEF AND ZUCCHINI LASAGNA

DIRECTIONS

12. In the meantime, let the oven preheat by setting the temperature to 375°F.
13. Take a deep glass baking dish and line it with parchment paper.
14. Further layer the bottom of the dish with 1/3 of the zucchini slices. Now evenly spread the meat mixture over the zucchini slices. Repeat the process with the remaining zucchini and meat mixture. (There should be a minimum of 3 layers.)
15. Sprinkle the shredded mozzarella on the top of the final layer.
16. Place the baking dish in the preheated oven and bake for about 35 minutes.
17. Once done, take the baking dish out of the oven and let it rest for about 10 minutes.
18. Serve hot!

Storage Tip: You can prepare this in advance and store it in an airtight container in the fridge. Before eating, simply heat it in the microwave.

BROCCOLI AND MARINATED STEAK

GENERAL INFO

Serving Size: 1
Servings per Recipe: 1
Calories: 309 calories per serving
Total Time: 1 hour and 10 minutes

INGREDIENTS

Lean beef – 4 ounces
Broccoli – 4 ounces
Soy sauce – 1 tablespoon
Balsamic vinegar – 1 tablespoon
Olive oil – 1 tablespoon
Pepper – a pinch

NUTRITION INFO

Fat – 16.9 g
Protein – 27.3 g
Carbohydrates – 12.7 g

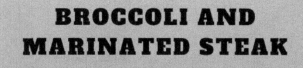

BROCCOLI AND MARINATED STEAK

DIRECTIONS

1. Start by taking a large bowl and adding in the balsamic vinegar, olive oil, pepper, and soy sauce. Mix well. Your marinade is ready.
2. Now slice the beef into strips measuring ½-inch thick.
3. Transfer the beef strips and marinade into a zip-lock bag. Mix well until well-coated.
4. Place it in the refrigerator for about 1 hour.
5. While the beef is marinating, clean the broccoli florets under running water.
6. Take a nonstick pan and place it on a medium-high flame.
7. Once the pan is hot enough, add in the marinated beef strips and broccoli florets and stir-fry for about 4 minutes.
8. Transfer onto a serving platter and serve hot.

Storage Tip: The dish can be made ahead of time and stored in a zip-lock bag or airtight container. It can stay in the refrigerator for up to 3 days. Make sure that you heat the dish nicely before eating.

EASY AND HEALTHY BEEF FAJITAS

GENERAL INFO

Serving Size: 1
Servings per Recipe: 4
Calories: 336 calories per serving
Total Time: 15 minutes

NUTRITION INFO

Fat – 16.8 g
Protein – 30.5 g
Carbohydrates – 10.6 g

INGREDIENTS

Beef strips (stir-fry) – 1 pound
Red onion (sliced) – 1 medium
Red bell pepper (seeded and sliced) – 1
Yellow bell pepper (seeded and sliced) – 1
Cumin powder – ½ teaspoon
Chili powder – ½ teaspoon
Splash of oil – as required
Salt – as per taste
Pepper – as per taste
Lime juice – ½ a lime
Cilantro (freshly chopped)
Avocado – 1

EASY AND HEALTHY BEEF FAJITAS

DIRECTIONS

1. Start by placing a cast-iron pan on a medium flame.
2. Once heated, add in the oil and let it heat through. Add in the beef strips and make sure there is breathing space between each strip. (Stir-fry in batches if necessary.)
3. Season each batch of beef strips generously and cook for about 1 minute on each side. Transfer the cooked strips to a bowl and keep it covered using a lid.
4. Place the same pan over the flame. Add the sliced bell peppers and onions to the meat juice that is remaining in the pan.
5. Sprinkle chili powder and cumin powder over the veggies and stir-fry until all the liquid is evaporated.
6. Take a serving platter and transfer the beef stir-fry strips and veggies to it.
7. Top with sliced avocado and garnish with chopped fresh cilantro.

Storage Tip: The beef strips and veggies can be stir-fried and stored in the refrigerator in an airtight container. These can be heated in the microwave before serving.

QUICK BISON MEATBALLS

GENERAL INFO

Serving Size: 5 meatballs
Servings per Recipe: 2
Calories: 271 calories per serving
Total Time: 20 minutes

INGREDIENTS

Ground bison – 8 pounds
Egg – 1
Garlic (finely chopped) – 2 cloves
Feta cheese (fat-free) – 0.4 cup
Onion powder – 1 tablespoon
Parsley (chopped) – 1 tablespoon
Dried oregano – 1 tablespoon
Salt – as per taste
Pepper – as per taste

NUTRITION INFO

Fat – 13.5 g
Protein – 33.7 g
Carbohydrates – 2.8 g

QUICK BISON MEATBALLS

DIRECTIONS

1. Start by taking a large mixing bowl and adding in the ground bison.
2. Add the finely chopped garlic, spices, and eggs to the bison. Mix well to combine.
3. Add in the feta and use your hands to gently fold it into the bison mix.
4. Divide the bison and feta mixture into 10 equal portions. Roll each portion into a ball.
5. Take a shallow skillet and grease it using cooking spray. Place the skillet over a medium flame.
6. Once the skillet is heated through, place the meatballs into it and let them cook for around 7 minutes. Keep turning them to cook them evenly on each side.
7. Once done, transfer the meatballs into a serving platter. Serve with salad, pita bread, or tzatziki.

Storage Tip: These meatballs can be stored in an airtight container in the refrigerator for up to 5 days. You can heat them in the microwave before eating

ROASTED VEGGIES WITH FLANK STEAK

GENERAL INFO

Serving Size: 1
Servings per Recipe: 6
Calories: 241 calories per serving
Total Time: 40 minutes

INGREDIENTS

Flank steak
Flank steak – 1.5 ounces

For the marinade
Lime juice – ¼ cup
Garlic (minced) – 1 clove
Ground ginger – ½ tablespoon
Red pepper flakes – ¼ teaspoon
Cumin – ¼ teaspoon
Salt – ½ teaspoon
Pepper – ¼ teaspoon

NUTRITION INFO

Fat – 11.5 g
Protein – 26.6 g
Carbohydrates – 8.3 g

For roasted veggies
Mushrooms (sliced) – 8 ounces
Grape tomatoes (halved) – 300 g
Zucchini (cubed) – 1
Coconut oil (melted) – 1 tablespoon
Cilantro (chopped) – 2 teaspoons
Lime juice – 2 tablespoons
Salt – ¼ teaspoon
Pepper – ¼ teaspoon

ROASTED VEGGIES WITH FLANK STEAK

DIRECTIONS

1. Start by taking a medium-sized mixing bowl. Add in the garlic, cumin, ginger, chili flakes, lime juice, pepper, and salt. Mix well to combine. Your marinade is ready.
2. Take a gallon zip-lock bag and place the flank steak inside it. Pour the marinade on the steak and seal the bag. Mix until the steak is fully covered.
3. Place the flank steak in the refrigerator and let it sit for about 30 minutes.
4. Set the temperature of the oven to 400°F and let it preheat.
5. Take a large baking sheet and place the mushrooms, zucchini, and tomatoes on it. Pour coconut oil on top and ensure the veggies are evenly covered.
6. Sprinkle pepper, salt, lime juice, and cilantro on top of the veggies. Mix well.
7. Place the baking sheet in the preheated oven and roast for about 10 minutes. Toss the veggies and roast for another 10 minutes.
8. In the meantime, let the grill preheat.
9. Take the flank steak out of the fridge and remove it from the bag. Place it on the preheated grill.
10. Grill the flank steak for about 10 minutes. Flip over and grill for another 10 minutes.
11. Once done, let it rest on a rack for about 10 minutes.
12. Slice the flank steak into ½-inch-thick slices and place the roasted veggies on top.
13. Serve hot!

Storage Tip: Once cooled, the steak and roasted veggies can be stored in separate airtight containers. They can be reheated on a grill or oven before serving.

poultry

RECIPES

CHICKEN AND CAULIFLOWER CASSEROLE

GENERAL INFO

Serving Size: 1
Servings per Recipe: 4
Calories: 288 calories per serving
Total Time: 40 minutes

NUTRITION INFO

Fat – 3.1 g
Protein – 40.6 g
Carbohydrates – 14.9 g

INGREDIENTS

Cooked chicken (shredded) – 1 pound
Red bell pepper (diced) – 1
Green bell pepper (diced) – 1
Salsa – 2 cups
Cauliflower rice – 3 cups
Egg – 1 large
Low-moisture cheddar cheese (shredded) – 1/3 cup
Low-moisture cheddar cheese (shredded) – 2 tablespoons
Cumin – 1 teaspoon
Paprika – ½ teaspoon
Limes – for topping
Cilantro – for topping
Extra-virgin olive oil cooking spray

CHICKEN AND CAULIFLOWER CASSEROLE

DIRECTIONS

1. Start by adding ¼ cup of water and cauliflower rice to a nonstick skillet. Place the skillet on a medium flame and cook for around 5 minutes.
2. Now set the temperature to 375°F and let the oven preheat.
3. While the oven is preheating, take a rectangular glass baking dish and lightly grease it with olive oil cooking spray.
4. Empty the cauliflower rice into a large mixing bowl and drain any excess liquid.
5. Add 1/3 cup of shredded cheddar and egg to the cauliflower rice. Mix well to combine.
6. Transfer the rice, cheese, and egg mixture to the prepared glass baking dish. Even out the top layer.
7. Place the baking dish in the preheated oven and bake for about 25 minutes.
8. While the rice is baking, take a nonstick skillet and toss in the diced bell pepper. Cook for about 5 minutes.
9. Now take a large mixing bowl and transfer the cooked bell peppers into the same. Also add in the shredded chicken, cumin, salsa, and paprika. Mix well to combine all the ingredients.
10. Take the baking dish out of the oven and evenly spread the prepared bell pepper and chicken mixture over the cauliflower rice.
11. Sprinkle the remaining cheese over the vegetables and place the dish back in the oven. Bake for about 7 minutes at 375°F.
12. Garnish with cilantro and lime. Serve hot!

Storage Tip: The casserole can be stored in the same glass baking dish if you cover it with cling film. You can reheat it in the oven before serving.

CHICKEN AND VEGGIE STEW

GENERAL INFO

Serving Size: 1
Servings per Recipe: 10
Calories: 111 calories per serving
Total Time: 45 minutes

NUTRITION INFO

Fat – 2.5 g
Protein – 10.1 g
Carbohydrates – 13.1 g

INGREDIENTS

Onion (chopped) – 2 cups
Cooked chicken breast (cubed) – 2 cups
Celery (chopped) – 1 cup
Tomatoes (whole, peeled) – 2 cups with liquid
Carrots (sliced) – 2 cups
Chicken broth – 5 cups
Sweet corn – 1 cup
Peas – 1 cup
Zucchini (sliced) – 1 cup
Cilantro – for garnishing

DIRECTIONS

1. Start by taking a large stockpot and placing it over a medium flame.
2. Now add in the chicken stock, chicken, tomatoes with liquid, celery, carrots, corn, zucchini, and peas.
3. Let it cook for about half an hour over a medium flame. Keep stirring while it cooks.
4. Once done, transfer into a serving bowl and garnish with cilantro.

Storage Tip: You can store the stew in an airtight glass container in the fridge for about 3 days.

LEMON-FLAVORED CHICKEN PICCATA

GENERAL INFO

Serving Size: 1
Servings per Recipe: 4
Calories: 269 calories per serving
Total Time: 30 minutes

INGREDIENTS

Chicken breasts (skinless and boneless) – 2
Unsalted butter – 3 tablespoons
All-purpose flour – 1½ tablespoon
White pepper – ¼ teaspoon
Salt – ¼ teaspoon
Olive oil – 2 tablespoons
Dry white wine – ⅓ cup
Chicken stock (low-sodium) – ⅓ cup
Lemon juice – ¼ cup
Capers (drained) – ¼ cup
Italian parsley (minced) – ¼ cup
Salt – as per taste
Pepper – as per taste

NUTRITION INFO

Fat – 15.6 g
Protein – 20.3 g
Carbohydrates – 3.4 g

LEMON-FLAVORED CHICKEN PICCATA

DIRECTIONS

1. Start by cutting both chicken breasts in half (lengthwise). Each breast should be about ½-inch thick. Flatten the breasts using a mallet if the breasts are thicker.
2. Take a shallow dish and add the all-purpose flour, pepper, and salt. Mix well.
3. Dredge all the slices of chicken breasts into the flour mix. Make sure to shake off any excess flour. Set aside.
4. Take a large cast-iron pan and place it on a medium flame. Pour in the olive oil and let it simmer.
5. Now place the chicken breasts in the pan and cook for about 4 minutes. Flip over and cook for another 4 minutes. Ensure that there is a nice brown crust on both sides of the breasts. Take the breasts out of the pan and set aside.
6. Pour the wine into the pan and stir well. Make sure to scrape out all the brown bits.
7. Add the chicken stock and lemon juice to the pan. Increase the flame to high and let it boil for 3 minutes. The sauce should begin to thicken.
8. Now reduce the flame to medium. Add the butter to the pan and stir well to combine.
9. Also, stir in the parsley and capers. Return the chicken breasts to the pan and let them heat through.
10. Transfer onto a serving platter and serve hot!

Storage Tip: Chicken breasts can be prepared in advance and stored in a glass airtight container in the fridge for up to 3 days. The dish can be reheated in a pan before serving.

TURKEY AND AVOCADO PATTIES

GENERAL INFO

Serving Size: 1
Servings per Recipe: 2
Calories: 249 calories per serving
Total Time:

NUTRITION INFO

Fat – 15.4 g
Protein – 26 g
Carbohydrates – 4.2 g

INGREDIENTS

Ground turkey, (93% lean) – 8 ounces
Avocado (chopped) – ½
Egg – 1
Garlic – 1 clove
Salt – as per taste
Pepper – as per taste
Olive oil cooking spray

DIRECTIONS

1. Start by taking a large mixing bowl. Add in the ground turkey, chopped garlic, egg, pepper, and salt. Mix well.
2. Now add in the chopped avocado and gently fold it with the turkey mixture.
3. Divide the mixture into 2 equal halves and mold each half into a patty.
4. Take a nonstick pan and grease it with olive oil cooking spray. Place the patties in the pan and cook for about 3-4 minutes on each side over a medium flame.

Storage Tip: These patties can be stored in zip-lock bags in the fridge. Just pop them into the microwave before serving.

TURKEY ROLLS WITH PECANS AND CRANBERRY

GENERAL INFO

Serving Size: 1
Servings per Recipe: 4
Calories: 177 calories per serving
Total Time: 5 minutes

NUTRITION INFO

Fat – 13.2 g
Protein – 7.2 g
Carbohydrates – 5.3 g

INGREDIENTS

Cream cheese (softened) – 4 ounces
Dried cranberries (chopped) – 2 tablespoons
Green onions (sliced) – 2 tablespoons
Toasted pecans (chopped) – 2 tablespoons
Turkey breast slices – ¼ pound

DIRECTIONS

1. Start by laying the turkey breast slice on a flat working surface.
2. Place 2 tablespoons of cream cheese on each turkey slice.
3. Sprinkle 1½ teaspoons of green onions, pecans, and dried cranberries on top of each turkey slice topped with cream cheese.
4. Hold one edge of the turkey slice and roll it up pinwheel-style. Repeat the process with the remaining slices.
5. Serve with the dip of your choice.

Storage Tip: Turkey rolls can be wrapped in cling film and stored in the refrigerator for later.

TUSCAN STYLE ROSEMARY CHICKEN

GENERAL INFO

Serving Size: 1
Servings per Recipe: 6
Calories: 187 calories per serving
Total Time: 30 minutes

INGREDIENTS

Butter – 3 tablespoons
Olive oil – 1½ tablespoons
Garlic – 3 cloves
Chicken breasts (boneless and skinless) – 3 large
Red wine vinegar – ½ cup
Salt – 1 teaspoon
Dry vermouth – 1 cup
Fresh rosemary – 3 tablespoons
Pink peppercorns – ¾ teaspoon

NUTRITION INFO

Fat – 11.4 g
Protein – 16.6 g
Carbohydrates – 0.9 g

TUSCAN STYLE ROSEMARY CHICKEN

DIRECTIONS

1. Start by cutting all 3 chicken breasts in half. Use a kitchen paper towel to blot any excess water from the chicken breasts.
2. Take a large nonstick skillet and place it on a medium-high flame. Add in the olive oil and butter.
3. Once the butter is melted, toss in the garlic cloves and let them cook for around 30 seconds. Remove the garlic cloves from the oil and discard.
4. Place the chicken breasts in the skillet and cook for 2 minutes. Flip over and cook for another 2 minutes.
5. Reduce the flame to medium. Pour the vinegar into the skillet and sprinkle with salt. Cover with a lid and cook the chicken breasts for another 5 minutes.
6. Now toss in the vermouth and rosemary. Let the chicken cook without the lid for around 10 minutes.
7. Transfer the chicken breasts to a platter and let the juices remain in the pan.
8. Add the peppercorns to the remaining juices in the pan and let the sauce boil for around 5 minutes. Make sure the sauce is slightly thickened.
9. Pour the prepared sauce over the chicken breasts and serve hot!

Storage Tip: You can cook the chicken breasts in advance and store in an airtight container in the fridge. You can store the sauce in a glass container. Heat the chicken in the skillet and heat the sauce in the microwave before serving.

vegetarian recipes

RECIPES

BLACK BEANS AND VEGGIE SOUP

GENERAL INFO

Serving Size: 1
Servings per Recipe: 4
Calories: 287 calories per serving
Total Time: 1 hour

NUTRITION INFO

Fat – 2.4 g
Protein – 17.2 g
Carbohydrates – 53.9 g

INGREDIENTS

Onions (diced) – 2
Carrots (diced) – 2
Celery (diced) – 3 sticks
Red bell peppers (diced) – 2
Garlic (finely chopped) – 3 cloves
Red chilis (de-seeded) – 2
Cilantro – ½ bunch
Bay leaf – 1
Dried oregano – 1 tablespoon
Black pepper (freshly ground) – 1 tablespoon
Sea salt – ½ tablespoon
Black beans (drained and rinsed) – 2 cans (15 ounces)
Boiling water – 1 quart
Tomato (finely chopped) – 1
Salad onion (finely chopped) – ½ small
Fresh juice of ½ lime

BLACK BEANS AND VEGGIE SOUP

DIRECTIONS

1. Start by removing the leaves and stalks from the cilantro. Finely chop the stalks and leaves. Set aside

2. Take a large saucepan and pour in 3 tablespoons of water. To this, add the carrots, onions, bell peppers, celery, red chilies, garlic, coriander stalks, oregano, bay leaf, sea salt, and pepper. Mix until well-combined. Cover the pan using a lid and let the veggies cook for about 10 minutes. Keep stirring.

3. Add the black beans and boiling water into the saucepan. Keep stirring.

4. Remove the lid from the saucepan and lower the flame. Allow the soup to cook for 30 minutes.

5. While the soup is cooking, make the lime salsa. For this, you will combine the tomato, salad onion, and cilantro leaves in a small bowl. Squeeze in the fresh lime juice.

6. Pour the soup in shallow bowls and finish by topping with lime salsa.

Storage Tip: The soup can be made ahead of time and stored stored in the refrigerator in a food-grade container. It can be heated right before eating.

CAULIFLOWER AND KABOCHA SQUASH SOUP

GENERAL INFO

Serving Size: 1
Servings per Recipe: 4
Calories: 125 calories per serving
Total Time: 30 minutes

INGREDIENTS

Olive oil – 2 tablespoons
Yellow onion (diced) – ½
Garlic (minced) – 3 cloves
Fresh ginger (minced) – 1 tablespoon
Cauliflower florets – 2½ cups
Kabocha squash (cubed) – 2½ cups
Ground cardamom – ½ teaspoon
Cayenne – ¼ teaspoon
Bay leaves – 2
Vegetable broth – 4 cups
Vanilla almond milk (unsweetened) – ½ cup
Salt – ½ teaspoon
Pepper – ¼ teaspoon

NUTRITION INFO

Fat – 7.7 g
Protein – 3.4 g
Carbohydrates – 11.6 g

CAULIFLOWER AND KABOCHA SQUASH SOUP

DIRECTIONS

1. Start by pouring the olive oil into a nonstick saucepan and placing it over a medium flame.
2. Toss in the onion, ginger, and garlic. Sauté for around 3 minutes.
3. Now add in the squash, cauliflower, cayenne, bay leaves, and cardamom. Mix well.
4. Pour in the vegetable broth and bring the vegetables and stock mixture to a boil.
5. Lower the flame and let the soup simmer for about 10 minutes.
6. Remove the pan and use the blender to puree the mixture.
7. Once the soup is pureed, return the pan to the low flame. Add in the almond milk. Mix well.
8. Finish by seasoning with pepper and salt.

Storage Tip: The soup can be stored in the refrigerator for 3 days. The soup can also be frozen and used for a couple of weeks.

CAULIFLOWER IN VEGAN ALFREDO SAUCE

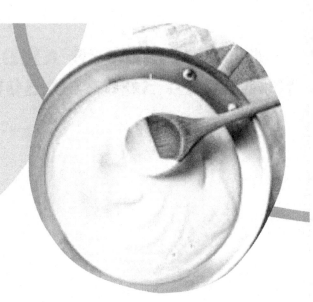

GENERAL INFO

Serving Size: 1
Servings per Recipe: 4
Calories: 138 calories per serving
Total Time: 15 minutes

NUTRITION INFO

Fat – 9.1 g
Protein – 3.9 g
Carbohydrates – 10 g

INGREDIENTS

Olive oil – 1 tablespoon
Onion (diced) – 1 medium
Garlic – 2 cloves
Cauliflower florets (chopped) – 4 cups
Vegetable broth – 1 cup
Lemon juice (freshly squeezed) – 1 teaspoon
Sea salt – ½ teaspoon
Nutritional yeast – 1 tablespoon
Pepper – as per taste
Vegan butter – 2 tablespoons
Chili flakes – 1 teaspoon
Zucchini noodles – for serving

CAULIFLOWER IN VEGAN ALFREDO SAUCE

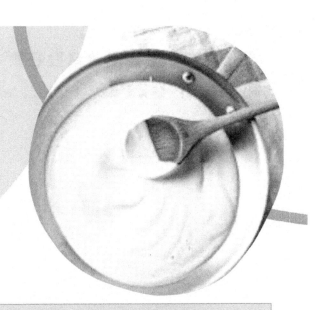

DIRECTIONS

1. Start by placing a stockpot on a medium-high flame. Pour in the oil and let it heat through.
2. Once done, toss in the diced onion and cook for about 4 minutes. The onion should be translucent.
3. Add in the garlic and cook for about half a minute. Keep stirring to avoid sticking.
4. Add in the vegetable broth and chopped cauliflower florets. Stir well and cover the stockpot with a lid. Let the cauliflower cook for around 5 minutes and then remove it from the flame.
5. Take a blender and transfer the cooked cauliflower into it. Pulse until the puree is smooth and creamy in texture. (Add 1 tablespoon of broth if necessary.)
6. Add salt, lemon juice, nutritional yeast, butter, chili flakes, and pepper to the blender. Blend until all the ingredients fully combine to form a smooth puree.
7. Place the zucchini noodles over a serving platter and pour the prepared cauliflower alfredo sauce over the noodles. Enjoy!

Storage Tip: The sauce can be stored in an airtight container in a refrigerator for up to 3 days. You can heat the sauce by adding a little water to get the desired consistency before serving. Pair the dish with any kind of vegetable noodles.

HEALTHY CARROT MUFFINS

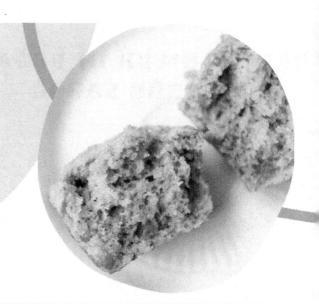

GENERAL INFO

Serving Size: 1
Servings per Recipe: 8
Calories: 189 calories per serving
Total Time: 40 minutes

NUTRITION INFO

Fat – 13.9 g
Protein – 3.8 g
Carbohydrates – 17.3 g

INGREDIENTS

Dry ingredients
Almond flour – 1¾ cups
Tapioca starch – ¼ cup
Granulated sweetener of choice –
½ cup
Baking soda – 1 teaspoon
Baking powder – 1 teaspoon
Cinnamon – 1 tablespoon
Nutmeg – 1 teaspoon
Cloves – ¼ teaspoon
Salt – 1 teaspoon

Wet ingredients
Coconut oil – 1/3 cup
Vanilla extract – 1 teaspoon
Flax meal – 4 tablespoons
Water – 1½ cups
Banana (mashed) – 1 medium
Carrots (shredded) – 1½ cups

HEALTHY CARROT MUFFINS

DIRECTIONS

1. Start by preheating the oven to 350°F.
2. Take a muffin tray and place paper cups in all the molds. Set aside.
3. Take a small glass bowl and add ½ cup of water and flax meal. Let this sit for about 5 minutes. Your flax egg is ready.
4. Take a large mixing bowl and add in the almond flour, tapioca starch, granulated sugar, baking soda, baking powder, cinnamon, nutmeg, cloves, and salt. Mix well to combine.
5. Make a well in the center of the flour mixture and pour in the coconut oil, vanilla extract, and flax egg. Mix well to form a mushy dough.
6. Now add in the shredded carrots and mashed banana. Mix until well-combined.
7. Use a spoon to scoop out an equal amount of mixture into 8 muffin cups.
8. Place the muffin tray in the oven and let it bake for about 40 minutes.
9. Remove the tray from the oven and let the muffins stand for about 10 minutes.
10. Remove the muffin cups from the tray and let them cool until they reach room temperature.
11. Serve!

Storage Tip: These muffins can be frozen in an airtight container for up to a few weeks. Heat them in the microwave before eating.

STEAMED KALE WITH MEDITERRANEAN DRESSING

GENERAL INFO

Serving Size: 1
Servings per Recipe: 6
Calories: 91 calories per serving
Total Time: 25 minutes

NUTRITION INFO

Fat – 3.5 g
Protein – 4.6 g
Carbohydrates – 14.5 g

INGREDIENTS

Kale (chopped) – 12 cups
Lemon juice – 2 tablespoons
Olive oil – 1 tablespoon
Garlic (minced) – 1 tablespoon
Soy sauce – 1 teaspoon
Salt – as per taste
Pepper (freshly ground) – as per taste

DIRECTIONS

1. Take a gas steamer or an electric steamer and fill the bottom pan with water. If using a gas steamer, place it on a high flame. If using an electric steamer, put it on the highest setting.
2. Once the water comes to a boil, add in the chopped kale and cover with a lid. Steam for about 7-8 minutes. The kale should be tender by now.
3. While the kale is steaming, take a large mixing bowl and add in the olive oil, lemon juice, soy sauce, garlic, pepper, and salt. Whisk well to combine.
4. Now toss in the steamed kale and gently fold into the dressing. Ensure the kale is well-coated.
5. Serve hot!

Storage Tip: Kale stays fresh in the refrigerator for up to 3 days. Ensure that you store the dressing and kale in different containers.

TOMATO AND ZUCCHINI SAUTÉ

GENERAL INFO

Serving Size: 1
Servings per Recipe: 6
Calories: 94 calories per serving
Total Time: 43 minutes

NUTRITION INFO

Fat – 2.8 g
Protein – 3.2 g
Carbohydrates – 16.1 g

INGREDIENTS

Vegetable oil – 1 tablespoon
Onion (sliced) – 1
Tomatoes (chopped) – 2
Zucchini (peeled) – 2 pounds and cut into 1-inch-thick slices
Green bell pepper (chopped) – 1
Salt – as per taste
Black pepper (freshly ground) – as per taste
Uncooked white rice – ¼ cup

DIRECTIONS

1. Start by taking a nonstick pan and placing it over a medium flame. Pour in the oil and let it heat through.
2. Add in the onions and sauté for about 3 minutes.
3. Now add in the zucchini and green peppers. Stir well and season with black pepper and salt.
4. Lower the flame and cover the pan with a lid. Let the veggies cook on low for about 5 minutes.
5. Once done, add in the water and rice. Put the lid back on and cook on low for at least 20 minutes.

Storage Tip: The tomatoes and zucchini sauté can be stored in the refrigerator for up to 4 days.

VEGETABLE NOODLES STIR FRY

GENERAL INFO

Serving Size: 1
Servings per Recipe: 4
Calories: 169 calories per serving
Total Time: 40 minutes

INGREDIENTS

White sweet potato – 1 pound
Carrots – 8 ounces
Zucchini – 8 ounces
Shallot (finely chopped) – 1
Garlic cloves (finely chopped) – 2 large
Red chili (finely chopped) – 1
Vegetable broth – 2 tablespoons
Olive oil – 1 tablespoon
Salt – as per taste
Pepper – as per taste

NUTRITION INFO

Fat – 3.7 g
Protein – 3.6 g
Carbohydrates – 31.2 g

VEGETABLE NOODLES STIR FRY

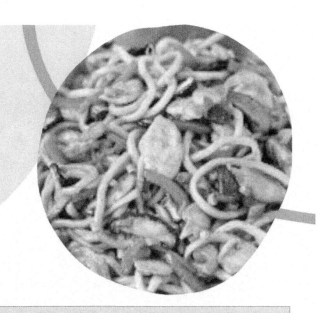

DIRECTIONS

1. Start by peeling the carrots and sweet potato. Use a spiralizer to make noodles out of the sweet potato and carrots.
2. Wash the zucchini thoroughly and spiralize it as well.
3. Take a large skillet and place it on a medium-high flame. Pour in the vegetable broth and let it come to a boil.
4. Toss in the spiralized sweet potato and carrots. Also add in the chili, garlic, and shallots. Stir everything using tongs and cook for a couple of minutes.
5. Transfer the vegetable noodles into a serving platter and generously season with pepper and salt.
6. Finish by drizzling olive oil over the noodles. Serve hot!

Storage Tip: The noodles stir-fry (except sweet potato) can be stored in a food-grade container for up to 3 days. The noodles can be heated in the microwave before eating. The sweet potato will stay fresh for consumption only until the next day.

seafood recipes

AHI POKE AND AVOCADO SALAD

GENERAL INFO

Serving Size: 1
Servings per Recipe: 4
Calories: 260 calories per serving
Total Time: 20 minutes

NUTRITION INFO

Fat – 21 g
Protein – 16.8 g
Carbohydrates – 8.4 g

INGREDIENTS

Sushi-grade ahi (diced) – ½ pound
Sesame oil – 1½ teaspoons
Soy sauce (low-sodium) – 1 tablespoon
Chili paste – 1 teaspoon
Rice vinegar – ½ tablespoon
Cooked bacon (diced) – ½ piece
Persian cucumber (diced) – ½
White sesame seeds – ½ tablespoon
Green onions (chopped) – 1 (only green parts)
Macadamia nuts (toasted) – ¼ cup
Seaweed salad – 2 tablespoons (optional)
Avocados – 2

DIRECTIONS

1. Start by taking a cast-iron pan and placing it over a medium-high flame. Once the pan becomes hot, add in the bacon. Cook until it becomes crisp.
2. Take a large glass mixing bowl and add in the soy sauce, sesame oil, rice vinegar, and chili paste. Mix well to combine.
3. Now toss in the bacon, ahi tuna, sesame seeds, bacon, macadamia nuts, seaweed salad, and green onion. Mix all the ingredients well.
4. Now cut the avocados into 2 halves and use a knife to remove the pits.
5. Use a spoon to scoop around 2 ounces of salad into each of the avocado halves.
6. Serve fresh!

Storage Tip: The salad can be stored in an airtight container in the refrigerator

BAKED SALMON SERVED WITH GARLIC BUTTER

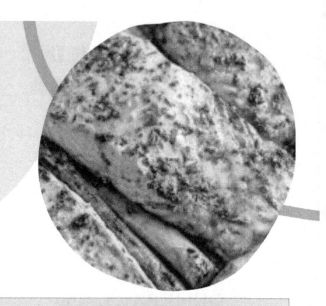

GENERAL INFO

Serving Size: 1
Servings per Recipe: 4
Calories: 350 calories per serving
Total Time: 20 minutes

INGREDIENTS

Unsalted butter (melted) – 4 tablespoons
Fresh garlic (minced) – 2 cloves
Fresh parsley (chopped) – 1 handful
Salt – as per taste
Pepper – as per taste
Lemon juice (freshly squeezed) – 3 tablespoons (extra for garnishing)
Salmon fillets – 4

NUTRITION INFO

Fat – 25.1 g
Protein – 28.6 g
Carbohydrates – 1.8 g

BAKED SALMON SERVED WITH GARLIC BUTTER

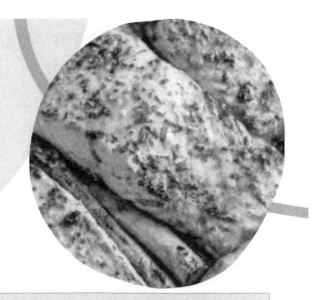

DIRECTIONS

1. Start by preheating the oven to 400°F.
2. Take a baking tray and line it with aluminum foil.
3. Take the salmon fillets and clean them thoroughly. Get rid of any visible bones.
4. Take a small mixing bowl and add in the garlic, melted butter, lemon juice, pepper, and salt. Whisk well to combine all the ingredients.
5. Place the cleaned salmon fillets on the lined baking tray. Make sure the skin side faces down.
6. Once done, generously brush the fillets with garlic butter. Make sure the fillets are perfectly coated with the butter.
7. Place the baking tray in the oven and bake for about 15 minutes. You do not need to flip the fillets halfway through.
8. Once done, take the baking tray out of the oven and brush the fillets generously with the prepared garlic butter.
9. Transfer the fillets onto a serving platter and drizzle with fresh lemon juice. Finish with a nice sprinkle of freshly chopped parsley.

Storage Tip: The baked fish can be stored in a food-grade container in the fridge for up to 3 days. The dish can be served with sautéed vegetables or any other side dish of your liking.

GRILLED SHRIMPS WITH YOGURT AND CHILI SAUCE

GENERAL INFO

Serving Size: 1
Servings per Recipe: 4
Calories: 134 calories per serving
Total Time: 20 minutes

INGREDIENTS

Shrimp – 1 pound
Plain Greek yogurt – ½ cup
Chili paste (sambal oelek) – ½ tablespoon
Lime juice – ½ tablespoon
Green onions (chopped) – for garnishing
Lime juice – for garnishing
Wooden skewers (soaked in water)

NUTRITION INFO

Fat – 2.3 g
Protein – 25.2 g
Carbohydrates – 2.4 g

GRILLED SHRIMPS WITH YOGURT AND CHILI SAUCE

DIRECTIONS

1. Start by removing the shells and thoroughly cleaning the shrimps. Carefully devein all the shrimps. Make sure to leave the tail on.
2. Skewer the shrimps by piercing through the center. You can place about 5 shrimps on each skewer.
3. Turn on the grill on a medium setting and place the skewered shrimps on the grill. Cook for about 3 minutes. Flip over and cook for another 3 minutes.
4. While the shrimps are cooking, prepare the yogurt and chili sauce. Take a glass bowl and add in the Greek yogurt, lime juice, and chili paste. Mix well to combine.
5. Transfer the cooked shrimps along with the skewers to a serving platter.
6. Squeeze fresh lime juice on top and garnish with chopped green onions. Serve with prepared yogurt and chili sauce.

Storage Tip: The shrimp can be stored in an airtight container in the refrigerator for up to 4 days.

SALMON AND SHREDDED POTATO PATTIES

GENERAL INFO

Serving Size: 1
Servings per Recipe: 12
Calories: 139 calories per serving
Total Time: 25 minutes

INGREDIENTS

Potatoes (peel and shred) – 3 medium
Eggs – 2
Salt – as per taste
Pepper – as per taste
Italian seasoning – 1 teaspoon
Flaked salmon (cooked) – ½ pound
Green onions (chopped) – 3
Capers (drained) – 2 tablespoons
Red bell pepper (chopped) – 1
Canned banana peppers (chopped) – ¾ cup
Fresh mushrooms (sliced) – ¾ cup
Dry bread crumbs – ¾ cup
Olive oil – 1 cup (for frying)

NUTRITION INFO

Fat – 4.6 g
Protein – 8.7 g
Carbohydrates – 15.9 g

SALMON AND SHREDDED POTATO PATTIES

DIRECTIONS

1. Start by taking the shredded potatoes and using a muslin cloth to squeeze out as much liquid as possible.
2. Once done, add the potatoes to a large mixing bowl. Also add in the eggs, pepper, Italian seasoning, and salt. Mix all the ingredients well. Ensure the potatoes are nicely coated.
3. Now add in the salmon, capers, banana peppers, red bell pepper, green onions, mushrooms, and dry bread crumbs. Mix until all ingredients are well-combined.
4. Divide the mixture into 12 equal portions. Form a round patty out of all the portions. The patties should be about ¾-inch thick.
5. Take a large anodized frying pan and place it on a medium-high flame. Add in the oil and let it heat through.
6. Once the oil is heated, add in the patties and fry for around 3 minutes. Flip over and fry for another 3 minutes. (Fry in batches if necessary.)
7. Line a plate with kitchen paper towels and place the fried patties on them. Pat dry any excess oil using a couple more paper towels.
8. Place the patties on a serving platter and serve with the dip or sauce of your choice.

Storage Tip: These patties can be cooled and stored in the refrigerator for about 2-3 days. Make sure you line the storage container with a paper towel to avoid moisture.

SHRIMP AND JALAPENO VEGGIE BAKE

GENERAL INFO

Serving Size: 1
Servings per Recipe: 4
Calories: 240 calories per serving
Total Time: 55 minutes

NUTRITION INFO

Fat – 9 g
Protein – 20 g
Carbohydrates – 8 g

INGREDIENTS

Shrimp – medium (peeled and thawed) – 15
Red onion (sliced) – 1/4 cup
Tomato (sliced) – 1 large
Zucchini (sliced) – 2
Jalapeño (deseeded and sliced) – 1
Cream – 1/3 cup
Eggs – 2
Melted butter – 1 tablespoon
Garlic (minced) – 2 cloves
Starch (gluten-free) – ¼ cup
Sea salt – as per taste
Black pepper – as per taste
Parmesan (grated) – ½ cup
Chili flakes – ½ teaspoon
Olive oil spray
Cilantro (chopped) – for garnishing
Chili flakes – for garnishing

SHRIMP AND JALAPENO VEGGIE BAKE

DIRECTIONS

1. Start by preheating the oven to 350°F.
2. Take a cast-iron pan and lightly grease it using olive oil spray. Layer the bottom of the pan with the onion, tomato, zucchini. and jalapeno.
3. Layer the shrimps on top of the vegetables.
4. Take a small mixing bowl and add in garlic, starch, cream, egg, and melted butter. Whisk well until the mixture is smooth.
5. Pour the cream and egg mixture over the shrimps and veggies. Season with pepper and salt as per your taste.
6. Top the shrimps with ½ cup of grated parmesan and finish by sprinkling chili flakes.
7. Place the cast-iron pan in the oven and let the shrimps and veggies bake for about 40 minutes.
8. Once done, take the pan out of the oven and season with more pepper and salt.
9. Garnish with chopped cilantro and chili flakes. Serve hot!

Storage Tip: This dish can be stored in the refrigerator for up to 3 days. Make sure that you use an airtight container.

SNAPPER FILLETS WITH PARSLE CELERY SALAD

GENERAL INFO

Serving Size: 1
Servings per Recipe: 4
Calories: 313 calories per serving
Total Time: 25 minutes

INGREDIENTS

Snapper fillets (wild-caught) – 4
Sea salt – as per taste
Pepper – as per taste
Celery sticks (washed and leaves removed) – 8
Flat parsley (destalked) – ½ bunch
Tahini – 1 tablespoon
Extra-virgin olive oil – 3 tablespoons
Fresh lemon juice – 2 tablespoons
Honey – ½ tablespoons

NUTRITION INFO

Fat – 15.6 g
Protein – 35.2 g
Carbohydrates – 6.3 g

SNAPPER FILLETS WITH PARSLE CELERY SALAD

DIRECTIONS

1. Start by preheating the oven to 350°F.
2. Take a baking tray and grease it using a few drops of extra-virgin olive oil.
3. Place the snapper fillet over the baking tray (skin side facing down). Sprinkle the fish fillets generously with pepper and sea salt.
4. Place the baking tray in the oven and bake for around 15 minutes.
5. While the fish is cooking, cut and remove the white part from the celery sticks. Further cut them into little sticks measuring about 1 inch long and 1/8-inch thick. Set aside.
6. Take the parsley leaves and clean them thoroughly. Once the leaves have dried, chop them coarsely. Set aside.
7. Take a glass bowl and toss in the cut celery and parsley. Mix well using your hands.
8. Take a glass bottle and add in the tahini, lemon juice, honey, and olive oil. Shake well to combine.
9. Take the fish fillets out of the oven and transfer them onto a serving platter.
10. Place parsley celery salad over the cooked fish and give it a nice drizzle of fresh lemon juice.
11. Serve hot with tahini dressing.

Storage Tip: The snapper fillets can be stored in an airtight container in the fridge for about 2 days. Make sure to store the celery and parsley salad in different glass containers. The dressing can be stored for up to a week.

TUNA AND AVOCADO SALAD

GENERAL INFO

Serving Size: 1
Servings per Recipe: 4
Calories: 225 calories per serving
Total Time: 5 minutes

NUTRITION INFO

Fat – 16.3 g
Protein – 13.9 g
Carbohydrates – 7.1 g

INGREDIENTS

Canned tuna (drained) – 10 ounces
Avocado – 1 large
Celery rib – 1
Fresh garlic – 2 cloves
Mayonnaise – 3 tablespoons
Red onion (peeled) – 1 small
Lemon juice (freshly squeezed) – 1 tablespoon
Cucumber – ¼
Parsley – 1 handful
Salt – ¼ teaspoon
Pepper – as per taste

TUNA AND AVOCADO SALAD

DIRECTIONS

1. Start by rinsing the cucumber, onion, celery, and parsley. Dry using a kitchen towel.
2. Finely chop the onion, celery, and cucumber. Also, very finely mince the garlic cloves. (You can use a garlic press, if handy.)
3. Take the avocado and cut it into 2 halves. Use a spoon to scoop out the pulp. Dice it into small pieces
4. Take a salad mixing bowl and add in half of the parsley, chopped onion, cucumber, celery, and minced garlic. Toss using a spoon.
5. Now add in the diced avocado and mayonnaise. Gently fold until all the ingredients are well-coated.
6. Season with pepper and salt as per your liking. Give the salad a gentle toss.
7. Serve in a bowl and garnish with reserved fresh parsley!

Storage Tip: The salad can be stored for up to 5 days in an airtight container in the refrigerator.

dessert
recipes

BANANA AND CHOCOLATE MUG CAKE

GENERAL INFO

Serving Size: 1
Servings per Recipe: 1
Calories: 237 calories per serving
Total Time: 6 minutes

NUTRITION INFO

Fat – 10.1 g
Protein – 19.7 g
Carbohydrates – 21 g

INGREDIENTS

Banana (ripe) – ½
Egg white – 3 tablespoons
Vanilla protein powder – ½ scoop
Oats – 0.2 ounces
Oat flour – 0.2 ounces
Cocoa powder – 1 teaspoon
Baking powder – ½ teaspoon
Stevia in the raw – 2 tablespoons
Olive oil cooking spray
Chopped walnuts – 0.3 ounces
Cooking spray

DIRECTIONS

1. Start by taking a large bowl and adding in the banana. Use a fork to mash the banana nicely.
2. Mix in the egg whites and use a whisk to incorporate it well.
3. Add the oat flour, protein powder, baking powder, oats, stevia, and cocoa to the banana and egg mixture. Mix well to combine.
4. Take a microwave-safe mug and grease it generously with a cooking spray.
5. Pour the batter into the greased mug and top with chopped walnuts.
6. Place the mug in the microwave and cook for about 1 minute.
7. Serve hot!

Storage Tip: The batter can be prepared in advance and stored for up to 2 days. Use a cling film to avoid oxidization.

BRAN, OAT AND BANANA COOKIES

GENERAL INFO

Serving Size: 1
Servings per Recipe: 12
Calories: 117 calories per serving
Total Time: 15 minutes

INGREDIENTS

Ripe bananas (mashed) – 2
Whole-wheat flour – ½ cup
Wheat bran – ¼ cup
Rolled oats – ¼ cup
Packed brown sugar – ½ cup
Plain yogurt (low-fat) – ½ cup
Maple syrup – 1/8 cup
Egg whites – 2
Ground cinnamon – 1 teaspoon
Salt – ½ teaspoon
Baking powder – ½ teaspoon
Raisins – ½ cup
Cooking spray

NUTRITION INFO

Fat – 0.5 g
Protein – 2.7 g
Carbohydrates – 27.6 g

BRAN, OAT AND BANANA COOKIES

DIRECTIONS

1. Start by preheating the oven to 350°F.
2. Take a cookie baking sheet and grease it using a cooking spray.
3. Take a medium-sized bowl and add in the mashed bananas, brown sugar, egg whites, yogurt, cinnamon, and maple syrup. Mix well.
4. Take the electric mixer bowl and add in the flour, wheat bran, oats, baking powder, and salt.
5. Turn on the electric mixer and gradually add the banana mixture. Keep running the mixer until all the ingredients are well-combined.
6. Add in the raisins and give it another mix. Now roll the mixture into table-tennis-sized balls.
7. Place the prepared cookie dough balls on the greased baking sheet.
8. Transfer the baking sheet to the preheated oven and bake for about 12 minutes.
9. Remove the sheet from the oven and let the cookies rest until they reach room temperature.
10. Once the cookies are done resting, place them in a vacuum container.

Storage Tip: The cookies can be stored up to a week in an airtight food-grade container.

CHOCOLATE BROWNIES

GENERAL INFO

Serving Size: 1
Servings per Recipe: 9
Calories: 210 calories per serving
Total Time: 43 minutes

NUTRITION INFO

Fat – 18.8 g
Protein – 3.6 g
Carbohydrates – 9.3 g

INGREDIENTS

Wet ingredients
Water – ½ cup
Vegetable oil – ½ cup
Greek yogurt (non-flavored) – ¼ cup
Vanilla extract – 1 teaspoon
Flax meal – 1 tablespoon

Dry ingredients
Coconut flour – ½ cup
Cocoa powder – ½ cup
Stevia – ½ cup
Baking soda – ¼ teaspoon
Salt – ¼ teaspoon
Chocolate chips (sugar-free) – ¼ cup
Walnuts (chopped) – ½ cup

CHOCOLATE BROWNIES

DIRECTIONS

1. Start by preheating the oven to 350°F.
2. Take a square (9-inch) baking tin and line it with baking paper. Use butter to grease all four sides of the baking tin. Set aside.
3. Take a medium-sized mixing bowl and add in the oil, vanilla extract, water, flax meal, and yogurt. Mix well to combine. Let the mixture stand for about 15 minutes.
4. The mixture should begin to thicken. Add in the cocoa powder, coconut flour, baking soda, salt, and stevia. Mix well to incorporate all the ingredients.
5. Add in the chopped walnuts and chocolate chips. Gently fold them into the mixture.
6. Use a spoon to scoop out the mixture and pour it into the baking tin. Make sure the mixture is smooth on top. Sprinkle some extra chocolate chips over the mixture.
7. Place the baking tin in the preheated oven and bake for about 15 minutes.
8. Take it out of the oven and let it rest at room temperature until it cools down.
9. Place it in the refrigerator for about 3 hours so that it sets completely.

Storage Tip: The brownies can be stored in an airtight container for up to a week in the fridge.

MOLTEN CHOCOLATE CAKE

GENERAL INFO

Serving Size:
Servings per Recipe:
Calories: 523 calories per serving
Total Time:

INGREDIENTS

Unsweetened chocolate (chopped)
– 4 ounces
Unsalted butter (cut in cubes) – ½
cup
Eggs – 2
Egg yolks – 2
All-purpose stevia blend – ¼ cup
All-purpose flour – 2 tablespoons
Salt – 1 pinch
35% whipping cream – ½ cup
All-purpose stevia blend – 1
teaspoon

NUTRITION INFO

Fat – 53.4 g
Protein – 9.3 g
Carbohydrates – 12.7 g

MOLTEN CHOCOLATE CAKE

DIRECTIONS

1. Start by preheating the oven to 400°F.
2. Take 4 oven-safe ramekins and grease them with butter.
3. Take a rimmed baking tin and place the butter ramekins into it. Set aside.
4. Take a pan and fill it with water. Place it over a medium-high flame and let the water come to a boil. Place a heatproof glass bowl over the boiling water and add in the chocolate and butter. Once the chocolate melts, set it aside.
5. Add the egg yolks, eggs, all-purpose flour, salt, and ¼ cup of all-purpose stevia blend to the electric mixer bowl. Mix until well-combined and the mixture is thickened.
6. Set the speed of the mixer to low and gradually add in the chocolate mixture. Keep the mixer running until all the ingredients are well-combined.
7. Pour an even amount of the mixture into all the buttered ramekins.
8. Place the baking tin in the preheated oven and bake for about 10 minutes.
9. While the cakes are baking, take a bowl and add in the whipping cream. Whip well until soft peaks begin to form. Add 1 teaspoon of all-purpose stevia blend to the whipping cream and whip for another minute.
10. Use a butter knife to loosen the edges of the cakes and place them on a quarter serving plate.
11. Top with a dollop of prepared whipped cream and serve!

Storage Tip: The batter can be prepared ahead of time and stored in the fridge for up to 3 days. Let it reach room temperature before you bake it.

RASPBERRY PUMPKIN MUFFIN

GENERAL INFO

Serving Size: 1
Servings per Recipe: 12
Calories: 217 calories per serving
Total Time: 1 hour

INGREDIENTS

Canned pumpkin puree – 1 cup
Coconut flour – ½ cup
Almond flour (blanched) – ¾ cup
Stevia – ½ cup
Tapioca – 3 tablespoons
Baking powder – 1 tablespoon
Cinnamon – 1 tablespoon
Nutmeg – a pinch
Salt – ¼ teaspoon
Eggs – 4 large (whites and yolks separated)
Coconut oil – ½ cup
Vanilla extract – 1½ teaspoons
Frozen raspberries – 1½ cups
Liquid stevia – 10 drops

NUTRITION INFO

Fat – 31.9 g
Protein – 4.8 g
Carbohydrates – 11.2 g

RASPBERRY PUMPKIN MUFFIN

DIRECTIONS

1. Start by preheating the oven to 350°F.
2. Prepare the muffin tin by placing muffin paper cups in all the molds.
3. Take a large mixing bowl and add in the almond flour, coconut flour, tapioca starch, stevia, cinnamon, baking powder, sea salt, and nutmeg. Mix well.
4. Now add in the pumpkin puree, egg yolks, coconut oil, vanilla extract, and stevia drops. Whisk until the flour mixture and wet ingredients are well-incorporated. The muffin batter is ready
5. Take another large bowl and add in the egg whites. Beat the eggs until you see stiff peaks being formed.
6. Transfer the frozen raspberries and beaten egg whites to the muffin batter. Use a spatula to gently fold the berries and egg whites into the batter.
7. Use a deep spoon to scoop out the batter and pour it into the lined muffin molds. Make sure you fill the muffin paper cups to the top.
8. Transfer the muffin tin to the preheated oven and bake for about 25 minutes. Insert a toothpick into the center to check if it comes out clean; if so, the muffins are perfectly baked.
9. Once done, take the muffin tin out of the oven and let the muffins cool for about 5 minutes.
10. Remove the muffins from the tin and let them cool until they reach room temperature.
11. Serve and enjoy!

Storage Tip: The muffins can be stored up to a week in the refrigerator so long as they are kept in an airtight container.

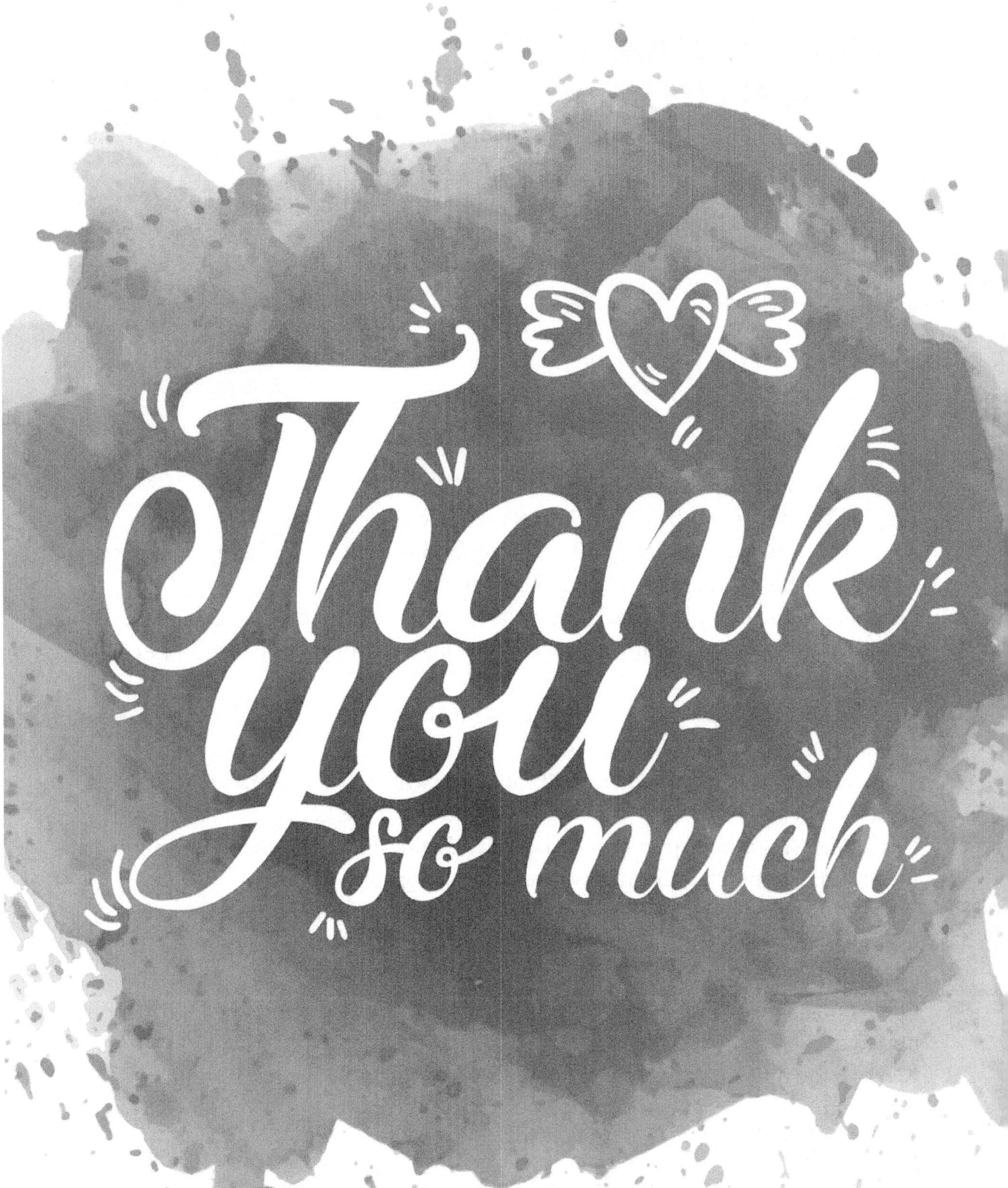
Thank you so much

New Generation
Poems from China Today

D1715417

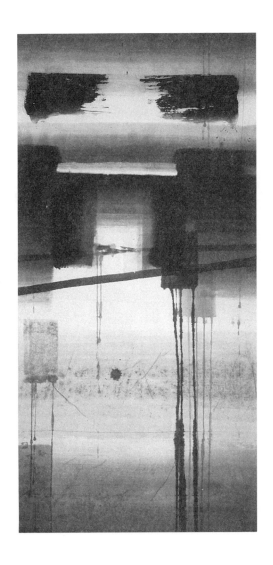

New Generation
Poems from China Today
Edited by Wang Ping

Translated by Wang Ping with Elizabeth Fox,
Ed Friedman, Lyn Hejinian, S.J. King, Gary Lenhart,
Dick Lourie, Murat Nemet-Nejat, Ron Padgett, David Shapiro,
Leonard Schwartz, Richard Sieburth, Jeff Twitchell-Waas,
Anne Waldman, Keith Waldrop, Lewis Warsh, and Zhen Zheng

Introduction by John Yau

Hanging Loose Press
Brooklyn, New York

895, 1
N

Published by Hanging Loose Press, 231 Wyckoff Street, Brooklyn, NY 11217-2208. All rights reserved. No part of this book may be reproduced without the publisher's written permission, except for brief quotations in reviews.

Printed in the United States of America
10 9 8 7 6 5 4 3 2 1

Hanging Loose Press thanks the Literature Program of the New York State Council on the Arts and the Fund for Poetry for grants in support of the publication of this book. The editor thanks the New York State Council on the Arts for a Translator's Fellowship.

Cover design and paintings by Shen Chen
Additional design by Caroline Drabik

Acknowledgments: Many of the poems in this anthology have appeared in the following literary journals: *The World, Tinfish, Talisman, River City: China: Here and There, Now and Then,* and *Manoa: The Zigzag Way.* Che Qiangzi's "Hand-copied Paperback" first appeared in *Xcp: Cross-cultural Poetics.*

Library of Congress Cataloging-in-Publication Data

New generation : Poems from China Today / edited by Wang Ping.
   p. cm.
   ISBN 1-882413-55-5. — ISBN 1-882413-54-7 (pbk.)
   1. Chinese poetry—20th century—Translations into English
I. Wang, Ping, 1957- . II. Title: Poems from China today
PL2658.E3N48   1999
895.1'15208—dc21   99-17919
                   CIP

Produced at The Print Center, Inc. 225 Varick St., New York, NY 10014, a non-profit facility for literary and arts-related publications. (212) 206-8465

Contents

The Poets and Their Translators

Note: Individual titles are given, and co-translators identified by initials, in cases where more than one of them worked on the poems of a particular poet.

Che Qianqzi
Zhen Zheng
Jeff Twitchell-Waas

Chen Dongdong
Wang Ping
S.J. King
Dick Lourie

He Zhong
(also known as Saldingnov)
Wang Ping
Lewis Warsh

Jia Wei
Wang Ping
Richard Sieburth

Liang Xiaoming
Wang Ping
Gary Lenhart

Liu Manliu
Wang Ping
Ed Friedman
David Shapiro
　　Mayfly's Journal DS
　　Autograph Book DS
　　As I Search for a Language EF
　　To Poets EF

Meng Lang
Wang Ping
David Shapiro

Mo Fei
Wang Ping
Leonard Schwartz
Lewis Warsh
   From "Words and Objects" LS
   The Sound of Chopping Wood LS
   Stuck in Place LS
   Coins Flung in Four Directions LS
   Young Prophet LS
   This Is Not the Last LW

Mo Mo
Wang Ping
Lewis Warsh

Tang Yaping
Wang Ping
Richard Sieburth

Wang Ping [originals are in English]

Wei Se
Wang Ping
Lyn Hejinian
Dick Lourie

Xi Chuan
Wang Ping
Murat Nemet-Nejat

Xue Di
Wang Ping
Keith Waldrop

Yan Li
Wang Ping
Lewis Warsh

Yi Sha
Wang Ping
Richard Sieburth

Introduction

*"The chair of poetry must remain empty, for poetry
does not collaborate with society, but with life."*

Frank O'Hara

by John Yau

In an interview[1] with the poet and translator, Arthur Sze,
Wang Ping made a number of useful observations about the
current state of contemporary Chinese poetry. The poets who
emerged in the wake of both the Tienanmen Square Mas-
sacre, which occurred on June 4, 1989, and the rise of the dis-
sident poets associated with the Misty School, many of whom
are currently living in the West, tend to be less idealistic, less
lofty in their language. The reasons for the younger genera-
tion's desire for what might be called "plain speech" are due
less to a generational shift than to a change in both political
and social circumstances. Rather than publishing and editing
in the relative openness that existed in the years preceding
Tiananmen Square, the current generation of experimental
poets is writing in a climate of extreme repression. Conse-
quently, while experimental poets of the earlier generation
often had print runs of 15,000, this generation has both fewer
outlets and less likelihood of reaching an audience of any size.
In the years before Tiananmen Square, Gu Cheng and Bei
Dao could make not only a living from writing poetry, but they
also began gaining a reputation abroad. Thus, the poets Wang
Ping has chosen to include in this anthology survive in a
repressive society with little hope of being read by either
those who share their mother tongue or by foreigners.

---

[1]Arthur Sze, "Writing in a Zigzag Way: An Interview with Wang Ping"
Manoa (Volume 10, Number 1, University of Hawaii Press, Honolulu,
1998), Editor: Frank Stewart, Feature Editor: Arthur Sze, pp 59-64

It is one thing to be a poet in a country that doesn't care about poetry, quite another thing to write poetry in a country where censorship makes it dangerous for both writer and reader. In America, poets can feel sorry for themselves, while in China self-pity would be an extravagance. And yet, what is self-pity but a desire for dignity? For whether one is a worker in an assembly plant or a person sitting in a room and writing, one wants to be afforded a certain amount of dignity for what one does. But perhaps dignity is not always something which is conferred upon the individual by an external source. Perhaps it is something that one can find through the writing itself. Certainly, Frank O'Hara's argument with the confessional poet Robert Lowell was about dignity. O'Hara thought Lowell was undignified to write about himself as he did, to repeatedly confess to feelings of impotence and isolation. He felt the older poet's articulations of self-pity were manipulative, that what Lowell really wanted, but never admitted, was power.

How do you resist both the tug toward self-pity and the desire for power? And, at the same time, how do you get beyond all the temptations to accommodate yourself? For one thing, the poet has to rethink what it means to be a poet. Given the long and central position poetry has held in Chinese culture, this is the daunting task the current generation is addressing both in their poetics and their poetry. Among other things, it means understanding one's relationship to both the past and the present, to a rich literary tradition and to a repressive political system.

Among their literary forebears, the contemporary Chinese poet has to address Lu Chi, who might be considered one of the founders of Chinese poetry. In his "Introduction" to his translation of Lu Chi's *Wen Fu: The Art of Writing*,[2] Sam Hamill writes:

---

[2]Sam Hamill, (translator) Lu Chi's *Wen Fu, The Art of Writing* (Minneapolis: Milkweed Editions, 1991) Page 11

"In the history of Chinese letters, Lu Chi holds a position similiar to that of Aristotle in the West, but with one paramount distinction: virtually every Chinese poet since the fourth century has gone to school on the Wen Fu, and most memorized it. He is revered by traditionalist and experimentalist alike."

Composed around 200 A.D., Lu Chi's *Wen Fu: The Art of Writing* is the first *ars poetica* written in China. After the "Preface," Lu Chi begins:

> The poet stands at the center of the universe,
>   contemplating the enigma,
> drawing sustenance
>   from masterpieces of the past.
> Studying the four seasons as they pass,
>   we sigh:
> seeing the inner-connectedness of things,
>   we learn the innumerable ways of the world.

Eighteen centuries later, in "The Brown Notebook: Rejecting Metaphor (Excerpts)," excerpts from which have been admirably translated by Wang Ping and Ron Padgett, Yu Jian writes:

> *We have forgotten language. Metaphor becomes a means of transportation. It disguises itself as poetry.*
> Language games becomes life games. Metaphor equals mask.
> Chinese culture is a 'metaphor culture.'
> *Poetry today rejects metaphor.*
> Real poetry rejects readers. It rejects the reading habit, not reading itself.
> Poetry is not a noun, but a verb.
> Poetry is its own reason for being. Poetry begins from language and ends in language.
> *Rejection and depth. Reject 'instinct,' 'inspiration,' or 'passion.'*

14

Writing "poetry begins from language and ends in language," it seems very likely that Yu Jian is being critical of Lu Chi's *Wen Fu: The Art of Writing*, and any poetic assertion regarding the poet's relationship to the universe.

Here, it is useful to recall a trajectory that begins in this century with Ezra Pound. Deriving his poetics from his study of Chinese ideograms, it was Pound who asserted that *sincerity* was "man-standing-by-his-word." While Pound is anti-metaphorical, he does advocate the use of clear, non-poetic images in poetry, a possibility which he was only able to fully formulate after he studied Chinese ideograms. After him, William Carlos Williams would go one step further and propose "No ideas, but in things." In order to go beyond the Modernist tradition of Pound and Williams with which he first identified, Robert Creeley would argue no ideas but in words. Thus, in 1960, Creeley wrote: "I mean then *words*—as opposed to content. I care what the poem says, only as a poem—I am no longer interested in the exterior attitude to which the poem may well point as signboard."[3]

Like Creeley, Yu Jian also wants to rid language of rhetoric, poetic devices, all the mechanisms meant to trigger a predictable response on the reader's part ("Real poetry rejects readers. It rejects the reading habit, not reading itself."[4]).

[3] Robert Creeley, "A Note," *A Quick Graph: Collected Notes & Essays* (San Francisco: Four Seasons Foundation, 1970) PP 32-33.

[4] Gao Minglu, Edited by, *Inside Out: New Chinese Art* (San Francisco: San Francisco Museum of Modern Art, New York: Asia Society Galleries, 1998), Exhibit catalog In "From Elite to Sma;; Man: The Many Faces of a Transitional Avante-Garde in Mainland China," Gao Minglu writes: "Wenda Gu, Wu Shan Zhuan, and Xu Bing were among the artists who created series of works or installations using Chinese characters." (Page 159). Common to all three artists is the desire to either disrupt or subvert language's capacity for reference. Gu restructures Chinese ideograms by reversing various components, writing them upside down. Zhuan juxtaposes "randomly selected phrases," and Bing "hand-carved more than two thousand wooden type elements," which he then printed. None of the characters in this project Book from the Sky (1987-91) can be pronounced.

Whereas Jack Spicer claims "No one listens to poetry," Yu Jian believes "Real poetry rejects readers." Clearly, Jian isn't preoccupied with the lack of audience; he doesn't derive his dignity from knowing how many readers he does or doesn't have. Thus, despite the very different circumstances in which "The Brown Notebook: Rejecting Metaphor (Excerpts)" was written, Yu Jian's desire to rid language of its capacity for illusion seems very familiar to us in the West. The particulars of the circumstances in which this desire is expressed are made all the more clear when we read "Individual" by Liang Xiaoming:

> You and I raise our mugs
> and drink our tea
> We smile at each other
> and nod elegantly.
> We're fastidious
> We talk about business,
> study our fingers,
> and express our opinions.
> Finally
> we walk our separate ways.
>
> At the gate we shake hands
> and look into each other's eyes.
> When we descend the stairs
> I wave at you
> if you're ahead of me
> and say "come again"
> Or if I'm the first
> you wave at me
> and say "walk slowly"
>
> Then we flee
> in different directions,
> and if it's raining
> we have our raincoats.

> (translated by Wang Ping and Gary Lenhart)

Think of all the poems Tu Fu wrote lamenting the immense distance between, or lack of communication from, his friend and fellow poet Li Po, and the lack of nostalgia, not to mention the highly circumspect state, the reader encounters in Liang Xiaoming's "Individual" becomes all the more poignant. Think of Ezra Pound's many translations of Tu Fu, which appear in *Cathay,* and one becomes more conscious of the origin of certain states of lamentation and self-pity that appear in many contemporary American poems. Aware as he so clearly is of Chinese literary tradition, Liang Xiao Ming also knows there is no turning back, no recourse to the past, which, if anything, has been embalmed by the present political situation.

The two nameless individuals might "smile" at each other, but there is a current of joylessness, and of the inability to celebrate this brief moment of meeting, that suffuses throughout the poem. And yet, what is remarkable about this poem, what makes it stand in stark contrast to both Classical Chinese poems and to much contemporary American poetry, is the poet's utter absence of self-pity, his rigorous refusal to lament his present circumstances, which we might remember is post-Tiananmen Square. At the center of his refusal is an unstated understanding of language, that it is something that is used either publicly or surreptitiously. One should, however, never confuse the two.

In "This Is Not the last," Mo Fei writes:

> I'm not the last
> person to be punished by language.
> The new wooden house
> gets knocked down by a tree
>
> The prisoner
> sets traps around himself.
> If he escapes alive,
> he'll take his crimes with him.

17

He has no other shortcut.
A knife blade separates life and death.
Light is cut open
and bent by the lonely sky.

The world is painful as fate.
Words are shackles.
Once he's learned how to confess
no one can ever defend him.

(Translated by Wang Ping and Lewis Warsh)

Surely, when Mo Fei writes "A new wooden house/gets knocked down by a tree," he is aware of Lu Chi's well known statement—"When cutting an axe handle with an axe,/ surely the model is at hand."[5] Mo Fei, however, is no utopian. Quietly, and without avant-garde fanfare, he has reversed Lu Chi's statement, for he knows that any agreement with it would amount to nothing more than a sentimental affirmation. Living in a post-industrial society, Mo Fei has experienced first hand what utopian thinking can bring to bear in the individual's daily life ("The world is painful...")

In contemporary China, language and the use of language does not exist apart from the individual's body. All concepts are likely to be empty unless one's body is also part of the equation. Thus, one has to stand by one's words, there is no other choice. This is what living in China after Tiananmen Square has made all too clear. Otherwise one lives in a web of lies and hypocrisy. This is the difference between the conditions under

---

[5] See Hamill, page 28, See also Gary Snyder, *Axe Handles* (New York: New Directions). In the title poem, Snyder refers to both Lu Chi and Ezra Pound. Snyder, a utopian, believes there are models near at hand. Thus, while American modernist tradition was originated in part by Ezra Pound, and his take on Chinese poetry and language, contemporary Chinese poets are responding to that very tradition from a different vantage point. Snyder sees himself as continuing a tradition, while Yu Jian and Mo Fei must seek an alternative to, as well as disrupt, their tradition. In this regard, they share something with avant-garde artists such as Wenda Gu and Xu Bing.

which Yu Jian wrote "The Brown Notebook: Rejecting Metaphor (Excerpts)" and those in which Pound claimed that the ideal state the poet should strive for is *sincerity*. Sincerity in Pound's time didn't necessarily get you condemned to jail or, as on the morning of June 4, 1989, wounded or killed. Thus, I would also make a distinction between Yu Jian's *ars poetica* and those made by various Americans connected with the Language movement. For the Language poets, many of whom have also rejected "metaphor," "instinct," "inspiration," and "passion," the primary concern is the social body. The difference is that "Chinese culture is a 'metaphor culture,'" while America's is one of exchange. One of the guiding principles behind Language poets's emphasis on the materiality of words is their belief that the social body, and all the places where the exchange occurs, is what the poet should address. In arguing that both author and narrative have died, and all so-called stories have been told, they are questioning the nature of meaning, which, after all, is a form of exchange.

In contrast to the Language poets, Yu Jian and his fellow poets cannot construct either a poetics or a poetry that exists apart from the individual body. This has nothing to do with either individualism or exchange. Rather, in China the individual body and the social body are synonymous in a way that they have never been in America. Consequently, Yu Jian and his fellow poets live in a state where any sanctioned exchange is at best a metaphor or illusion. They must write in what Wang Ping calls the "zigzag way."

"The world," Mo Fei tells the reader, "is painful as fate./ Words are shackles./ Once he's learned how to confess/ no one can ever defend him." Mo Fei knows he isn't the first or "last person to be punished by language." It may be an old story that he is telling us in plain words, but it certainly isn't one we have listened to very well. Perhaps it is time that we do listen, hear what these poets are saying that we have not heard before. In

her selection of poets and poems, Wang Ping, along with her co-translators, many of whom have already distinguished themselves as both poets and translators, brings us the news. What we might learn from reading this news is that poets writing in one of the world's oldest languages have much to tell us about the kind of measures one must use to stay alive. Foremost among those measures is recognizing all the uses that language, and those who use it, can be put to. As Robert Creeley put it: " At some point reached by us, sooner or later, there is no longer much else but ourselves, in the place given us."[6] Wang Ping's anthology *New Generation* brings us poems from that place, which is equally part of this world.

---

[6] Robert Creeley, "A Note on the Local," *A Quick Graph: Collected Notes & Essays* (San Francisco: Four Seasons Foundation, 1970), Page 34

Preface

by Wang Ping

1

This anthology is intended to introduce American readers to some of the important Chinese avant-garde poets who have emerged since the early 1980s. The term "new generation" is used in China to describe these poets and others. It is an accurate term historically; these are newer, younger poets. But it's important to note that the new generation includes poets whose work is very diverse in content, tone, and style. What they share and how they differ can be best understood in reference to an earlier movement, the "Misty poets," and to the vast changes—social, political, economic—that have taken place in China.

In the late nineteen-seventies, a number of poets rebelled against the official artistic ideology which held that art must serve politics and the people. They believed that the socialist reality had been so contaminated by excessive ideological propaganda that ideology had become a kind of simulacrum serving, as the poet Yang Xiaobing put it, "to alienate the human being from his or her true self." [1]

For the poets of the "Misty" or "Obscurantist" school of this first post-Mao generation, the function of poetry was first of all to recover and refine the human self. This emphasis was put into poetic practice through imagistic language. Landscape was viewed anthropomorphically, and poetry became a mirror with which to see oneself. By infusing landscape (sky, rain, mist, river) with personal emotions through an impressionistic prism—and often turning these images into political allegories—the Misty poets strove to transcend the confines of realism and create a new identity linked with both the self and the external world.

---

[1] Leo ou-Fan Lee, introduction, *The Red Azalea*, Edward Morin (ed.), Honolulu: University of Hawaii Press, 1990, p. xxvii. Other prominent "Misty school" poets include Bei Dao, Mang Ke, Shu Ting, and Yang Lian.

21

Poems of the Misty school invoked images of youth either as tragic, lonely heroes and martyrs fighting for humanity and freedom in opposition to the old world; or as pure, innocent youths aspiring towards truth, beauty and perfection. These poets were unified by their rebellion against falsehood and ugliness, and their single-minded belief in humanity. A resemblance might be seen here to the European Romanticism of the early nineteenth century.

Some of the poets in this anthology were, in the early eighties, younger adherents of the Misty school. They and others came to oppose the Misty school belief in "heroism" and the "imagistic" method of writing. The critic Leo ou-Fan Lee notes that they criticized their predecessors "for being too historically conscious and too ornate in their poetic imagery." [2] And in a 1988 article, Zhu Linbo characterizes the new generation poets as dissatisfied with the values, ideology and art of the existing world, and lists six of their "antis": anti-tradition, anti-sublimity, anti-lyricism, anti-culture, anti-aesthetic, and anti-poetic. [3]

This anarchistic attitude found its source partly in the climate of the times. In the years following Mao's death, the following revelatory one-liner was making the rounds among Chinese intellectuals: "Under the leadership of the Communist Party, we are advancing from socialism towards capitalism." The premise of the joke is, of course, the numerous contradictions that had arisen between China's old Maoist identity and its new reformist self.

During the 1980s, China was marked by the diminishing of state production and the rapid growth of production by pri-

---

[2] ibid.

[3] Zhu Linbo, "The Six Anti-Attitudes and Three Characteristics of the Third Generation Poets," *Youth Poetry Review* No. 2, 1988. There is some similarity here to the start, in the late fifties, of the beat movement in poetry and other areas of culture in the US.

vate and collective enterprises. According to a 1992 New York Times article, one percent of China's GNP in 1981 comprised private industrial output; the figure for collective enterprise was 21 percent; the state sector accounted for the other 78 percent. By 1991, the figures were 11 percent private and 36 percent collective, while state production had been reduced to 53 percent.[4] With the government all the while insisting that it was not abandoning socialism but perfecting it, China had begun to develop a consumer-oriented, market economy. Within the framework of a planned economy, the three stages of capitalism—market, monopoly, and multinational capital— were growing simultaneously. The gap between current reality and the fiction of Maoist socialism was giving China a sort of political, economic and cultural split personality.

Not surprisingly, the decade also saw the weakening of socialist ideology in China. The industrialization promoted by the government would inevitably lead not to the creation of the "new socialist person" but to the emergence of a "new cosmopolitan person," one who demanded more wealth, more individual freedom, more political rights.

Defending itself against the inevitable, the Party undertook a strategy that has more or less continued until today, launching one "socialist spiritual civilization" movement after another to stave off "bourgeois liberalization." This error they define as breaking from party leadership and straying off the socialist road mapped out by orthodox Marxist, Leninist and Maoist thought.

But socialism has been harder to define, and so has the Party's idea of socialist spiritual civilization. "Truth comes from practice," "Walk a step and look a step," "Proceed from facts"—these slogans, which the Party has been espousing since the eighties, have become, by default, a kind of frag-

---

[4] Nicholas D. Kristof, "Chinese Communism's Secret Aim: Capitalism" *New York Times*, Oct. 19, 1992: p. A6.

mentary, post-hoc pseudo-ideology. They apply exclusively to practical application and have in fact blurred the boundaries between what is considered correct and incorrect thinking and behavior.

The ideological void has been quickly filled by the products of Western, mostly American, cultures: disco, movies and videos, fashions, golf and horse racing, cosmetic surgery. As Frederic Jameson has noted, the expansion of multinational capital "ends up penetrating and colonizing those very pre-capitalist enclaves," including socialist China.[5]

But no matter how tattered the socialist system and its ideology have become, Party leaders maintain their refusal to countenance any overt reference to its sad condition. They stubbornly insist that China is still a communist country, and they continue to fill the airwaves with socialist slogans. These ideological assertions have degenerated into little more than a decorative art, equivalent to the arranging of banners and the beautification of whatever the government wants to do. At the same time the political leadership of the country continues to exacerbate the situation by promoting ever greater economic change.

The resulting atmosphere has created such perplexing uncertainty and confusion that cynicism and materialism have begun to emerge as part of Chinese life. It's against this background that the new generation of poets has emerged, trapped between their rejection of communist ideology and their distaste for the relentless advance of capitalist mass culture. Faced with such uncertainty, and with threats to their own identity, they have expressed the urgent need to find a foothold in a local and global environment undergoing constant and rapid transition.

---

[5]Frederick Jameson, *Postmodernism: Cultural Logic of Late Capitalism*, Chapel Hill: Duke University Press, 1991, p. 49.

2

While the young new generation poets have shared a common commitment to change what had gone before, their approaches are anything but unified. In what might be seen as an ironic echo of Mao's "hundred flowers" blooming, and in stark contrast to the single unitary voice of the Misty school, the early to mid-eighties witnessed an explosion of poetry schools and -isms among the younger poets who were later dubbed the new generation. Women emerged as an important force, and voices of minority ethnic groups gave expression to their individual cultures.

Many of the poets in this anthology were members or founders of these movements. Yu Jian was the leading member of two groups, They and College Students Poetry, which announced that its only aim and method was to "break," "smash" and "shatter" the concept of "sublimity" and "image" in poetic practice.[6] In Shanghai, Chen Dongdong, Mo Mo, Meng Lang, and Liu Manliu belonged to the Poetry Group on the Sea (a pun: "on the sea" is "hai shang"—Shanghai backwards). This group viewed poets as lonely craftsmen of language.[7]

Xue Di joined the Yuan Mingyuan Poetry Group, which was founded after the demise of the Misty school poetry magazine, *Today.* The name "Yuan Mingyuan" indicated that the members aimed to develop new poetry on the ruins of the old (in this case the Misty poetry).[8] This group lasted only a year, but the readings it organized, accompanied by music and light shows were attended by thousands of enthusiastic fans. In many ways these events were like American rock and roll con-

---

[6]Xu Jingya, Meng Lang, eds., *A Panorama of Chinese Modernist Poetry Groups,* Shanghai: Tongji UP, 1988, pp. 85-86.

[7]ibid, pp. 70-71.

[8]Yuang Mingyuan was an imperial palace garden in the western suburbs of Beijing. British and French forces raided and burned the palace in 1860.

certs. Extremism, the group to which Liang Xiaoming belonged, began in 1985. These poets declared that a pile of garbage was more real than a pile of gold because the garbage was closer to the truth of life. And the female poets of this generation—among them Jia Wei, Tang Yaping, Wei Se, Zhai Yongming, Zhang Er, Zhang Zhen, and Zhao Qiong—bear witness to their pain as women as well as artists.

Most of these schools and -isms were in fact more like poetry communities or groups, often with no more than ten members. They criticized their predecessors, pointing out that Misty school poetic devices and uses of language were no longer sufficient to express the frustration, confusion, anxiety, and despair of Chinese youth. The young rebels wanted to strip poetry of all social or cultural armoring as well as all myth and tragedy, in order to create a poetry that was free and pure. They had their own slogans and manifestos and each published its own mimeographed magazines. They had talent and energy and commitment.

The decentered and fragmentary quality of this poetry scene certainly reflected the energy of the reaction against the Misty school. But it may also have represented the new poets' way of rebelling against the traditional Chinese nostalgia for clarity, wholeness, and the sensible, a nostalgia for which China has paid an enormous price.

Historically, Confucianism, the long-held orthodox way of thinking, whose function was to tame wildness and to create docile and obedient subjects, had ill prepared the Chinese for the swirling currents of thought that entered the country starting about 1900. Confucianism gave way to Marxism, Leninism, and Maoism; these in their turn helped train loyal believers to better serve the Communist Party and its cause. The subsequent decline of communist ideology in the 1970s and 1980s led to the ideological vacuum discussed earlier. The clock could not be turned back to Confucianism; flux and confusion ruled.

For the new poets, the ideals of Misty poetry had also failed. Though aimed at reclaiming individualism, the movement, they thought, had eventually just hardened into a new orthodoxy. Given the failure of so many systems and ideologies, it is not surprising to find the birth in 1986 of a leading avant-garde poetry group who named themselves and their magazine Fei Fei——literally, and simply, "No No."

3

Although readers of this anthology might not immediately find a distinctly unified voice of "avant-garde Chinese poetry," still, taken as a whole the new generation poets do show us something about poetry in China today, and about the country itself.

And there are important things they do share with one another. To the poets of the new generation, the Misty poets, their single-minded belief in truth, perfection, and humanity (which may remind us again of Keats and the other Romantics), and their imagistic, symbolic poems seemed hopelessly outdated and irrelevant. For the new generation, the crucial task was not to celebrate heroism and utopian idealism but to reconnect with reality by destroying the facades of decency, beauty, and sublimity which were obscuring language and art. Their poems demonstrate an emphasis on the darkness and ugliness of human nature; on breaks and discontinuities rather than linear narrative (here they are modernists); on gaps and holes rather than seamless webs; on difference rather than commonality. Their shared goal has been, in general, to re-establish a more "pure" relationship between words and objects, in reaction against both the impractical romanticism of the Misty poets and the sloganeering degradation of language that accompanied the weakening of socialist ideology.

And all the new poets are fully aware of both the indispensability of language and the difficulty of using it truthfully.

"Poets live in language," writes Mo Fei in a letter to me, but "the nature of language is to obscure." Thus to cleanse the language of "garbage," to restore the naming power of words and call things by their proper names, has become the most crucial task. Mo Fei again: "The problem of poetry is how to deal with the relation between words and objects." These poets seek pure language, renouncing any symbolic "meaning" or imagistic juxtaposition that their Misty poet predecessors have, in their view, forced onto words.

Many of them also share an ambiguous attitude toward their own cultural and literary tradition. On one hand is their hostility toward what they see as conservatism, lifelessness, and oppression. Yet often it seems nothing much is left of the past anyway but ruins, a wasteland of abandoned ideology, and the rapid collapse of both nature and culture under the weight of capitalism and the false culture that accompanies it. And, as poets, they can never make a complete break, since they rely on language, which itself is a crystallization and product of Chinese tradition. The problem of how much to keep and how much to let go is thus enduring and agonizing.

Another common thread involves the attitude of these poets to a tradition not their own—they share an exposure to and an interest in Western literature and philosophy. Many of them wrote their first poems after reading Whitman, Rilke, or other Western poets, and many, especially the women, were influenced by American confessional poets, most notably Sylvia Plath and Robert Lowell. Thanks to the availability of good translations in China, new generation poets now have access to classical as well as 20th century world literature, philosophy, literary theory and criticism.

Finally, the poets' biographies demonstrate the complexity and variety of their lives and work. Most still live in China. A few have emigrated to the US. As do poets in other countries, they occupy a wide range of professions, the writing of poetry

being a notoriously poor provider of income worldwide. They speak to us as individuals and artists who share things in common and who have great differences; and they speak to us as representatives of a country and culture very different from our own, which nevertheless offers surprising flashes of familiar feelings and observations.

And the term "flash" is appropriate for another reason. The movements, schools, poetic communities of the eighties were short-lived, but they brought about significant change, and their impact is still being felt on Chinese poetry. And of course the poets themselves, those who were part of that evanescent but brilliant scene, are still writing. Thus it seems fitting to close this introduction with a quote from Liu Manliu. It seemed to us that his "Mayfly's Journal" can be viewed in part as a comment on the brilliant intensity of art, however fleeting, and its insistence that we pay attention. "We live our lives as you take vacations," says the narrative persona of the poem; "in one day we mate, lay eggs, and die./ Our flight is without limits."

On the Translations

When I undertook these translations, I saw my main tasks as finding the poet's intended effect, then conveying that effect—and the form of the original—as accurately and clearly as possible. I collaborated on the translations with twelve American poets: Elizabeth Fox, Ed Friedman, Lynn Hejinian, S.J. King, Gary Lenhart, Murat Nemet-Nejat, Ron Padgett, David Shapiro, Richard Sieburth, Anne Waldman, Keith Waldrop, and Lewis Warsh. Their dedication and hard work in assembling this anthology has been invaluable, and I wish to express my gratitude to all of them.

I found that teamwork made the task both more challenging and more interesting. In my own first drafts I sought to be

as understandable as possible in English while remaining as close as I could to the original. The American poets then read them and marked everything which seemed to them unclear, hackneyed, or incomprehensible.

Following these two "passes" at the material, I would meet with each collaborator to go over the remaining problems. These were meetings marked sometimes by smooth agreement and sometimes by clashes, between original and translation, Chinese and American cultures and languages, and the diverse personalities and poetic tastes of the collaborators. Whatever the individual case, the end result has, I think, been a successful set of translations which are true to the Chinese originals. When the manuscript of the book was being edited for publication, a final step in the translations was my collaboration with poet and Hanging Loose editor Dick Lourie.

It's our hope that in our efforts we have approached the ideal expressed by Walter Benjamin: "A real translation is transparent; it does not cover the original, does not block its light, but allows the pure language, as though reinforced by its own medium, to shine upon the original all the more fully." [9]

My special thanks go to Lewis Warsh, who gave me unconditional support throughout this project; to Professor Tim Reiss at New York University's Department of Comparative Literature, who gave very helpful suggestions and criticism to the work as my master's thesis advisor; to Yan Li, editor of *First Line,* who introduced me to many poets whose work is included in this anthology; to Zou Jingzhi, who helped me locate and relocate many of the poets in China; to Arthur Sze, who helped read the manuscript and introduced many of the poets in the anthology to *Manoa* magazine, which ran excerpts from this collection; to Ed Friedman and Walter Lew, who

---

[9] Walter Benjamin, "The Task of Translator," *Illuminations,* Hannah Arendt (ed.), 5th edition, New York: Schocken Books, 1978, p. 81.

helped me with the NYSCA grant; to Adam Lerner for his help with the contracts, to Donna Brook and Bob Hershon, who are such a pleasure to work with; to Mark Nowak, editor of *Xcp*, who agreed at the last minute to let me include Che Qianzi's poem in the anthology; to all the co-translators for their generosity, enthusiasm, and talents. Finally, I want to thank Dick Lourie, who worked on the final edition of this project with keen devotion, whose exquisite ear for music made the poems more subtle and much sharper, and who helped clarify the ideas in this preface.

31

《傳抄紙本》璧頁

車前子

（1999年1月21日復製於北京）

前言：許多年來，有个秘密組織在亞洲一帶尋找《傳抄紙本》。据说凡是醉到手的话，就可了知治国平天下的奥妙。于此同时，也有一个秘密組织，他们否认的是存在，但为了不让诸学者失望，又一直在仿托着《傳抄纸本》这却著作。而这里的《傳抄纸本》，是我从想象和猜想的某些书籍中抄录的化所。前化。后面。与诸书志同者的《傳抄纸本》无关，和仿托者阿援的《傳抄纸本》*

* 此页复制——传抄品，依据的是手边的版本，与翻译者所使用的版本有些微不同

Born in Suzhou, Jiansu Province, in 1963, Che Qianzi now lives in Beijing. He is the author of several collections of poetry and prose, including *Three Primary Colors*. His latest works are the poetry sequences "Numbered Musical Notation" and "Hand-Copied Paperback," the latter of which is presented here.

传抄纸车　　　　　中国（送一）

33 71　……出十宫中国）……　　（许·三〇）

33 72　……口其邑口其时……

33 85　……务以行争犯……

33 94　凡此……

34 14　……口民口口……

34 26　……奈伊　（许·四六）

34 38　……口所其引）（阴·一二）

34 76　……金　（阴·三）

34 77

35 19　……下口口口……

35 53　有口……

35 70　·三……

Hand-Copied Paperback

1. Background

Preface: For many years, a secret society in Southeast Asia has been searching for a book entitled *Hand-Copied Paperback*. It is said that with this book in hand, one would have the secrets of running the country at their fingertips.
However, at the same time, there exists another secret society which does not believe such a book exists. But in order not to disappoint the book-hunters, they have forged a *Hand-Copied Paperback*.
This *Hand-Copied Paperback* contains excerpts copied from other works. Cards. One-sided. Unrelated to either *Hand-Copied Paperback* that the book-hunters look for or to those making the forged book. Crucial. Urgent.

Stylistic musical works culture is a kind of copying process in it there are many slips of the pen and parts left out when we open our eyes and want it is just like the "descendants passing off modern works as ancient."

Wittgenstein says: "Culture is a kind of hobby, a hobby founded on copying."

What a person copies may be what he himself left out

My head knows nothing of what my hand is writing down

Culture, —handwritten forms.

Afterword: fake book fake money fake man;
                  true theory true story true stuff

Appendix: For my part the *Hand-Copied Paperback* is completed — or rather half completed. For the other half, I will invite 99 people with different levels of education to copy it.

CHE QIANZI

The copying process will be as follows:
The second person copies my original; the third person copies
the second person's; the fourth copies the third. And so on.
When it is time, I will make a comparative study of the 99
copies.
I expect to find some interesting variations and ways of trans-
formation.
The deadline set down for the process is ten years.

2. Text

Hand-Copied Paperback   India
    egg egg shell   carrying stones   stone blocks
                                piled up into a temple
            dust billows up   in the process
                gently floats
            sulfure epic aerial combat
as armies of monkeys march along roads as armies of
monkeys march along treetops hand-copied tomes, portray
the witness

Hand-Copied Paperback   Tibet
                      amazing   clouds
                      amazing   Gesang
        yellow robes, plumpen in the sun
yellow crown   love-songs

        fresco:
        high up, only approached by crawling

black and white documentary
better than a dozen actors, sorcerers enter the city
        black and white documentary:
    the blue mountains and green rivers in Chinese culture

36

not the blue and green people sitting or flying in Chinese
   culture
we danced the whole night the whirling tube whirling and
   whirling

Hand-Copied Paperback   Japan
   beauty of rice paper   craftsman meticulously uphold-
                               ing the art of paper making
   who are you?   using false names/*kana*
   real grass,   ____ half the alfalfa field is purple
   upright character, unrestrained behavior
   "solitude"
father and brother build a wall at home, double-petaled cher-
ries bear flowers but not fruit
interested in sorcerers at the same time
                               red white cherries   geisha

   sage seeds
   vanity grass
   the monk's tale
      cannot help being amazed at the blankness of a piece
         of paper

Hand-Copied Paperback   Ceylon

   that which can be destroyed by fire, can be destroyed by
      water
   the most fragile can best preserve humanity
                                     out of convenience
   towering athenaeums, library domes
   dream of a manuscript, era of printing
      from then on, facilitates exchange
racer no. 185 first reaches the history of paper

CHE QIANZI

Hand-Copied Paperback   Thailand
    mistakes coax people into storing filled with mistakes high
        prices
    smart people's height grows, people grow, lazybones
    shorten their bodies
    lazybones short   short riders
               passes over the shoulder:
                  squatting on the shoulder
                  a cat or a lion

    lingering warmth

    monkey trainer in the warehouse doorway, the one on duty
        hooks the ladder
    leaning against a wall, bits of a broken glass stuck on it
             like a dentist

"open your mouth, and legs, hmmm, ok."

Hand-Copied Paperback   Burma

    Burmese child   shy Burma
    9-year old adult   strict monastery rules   silver pagoda tops
    like an antenna wave long wave short   dangerous big ships
    women carry on their heads men holding chickens
                  frequency modulation   stereo
    three dimensional cartoons   small bird and the king
Buddha crosses river, does not get wet, not that the river is
       not wet

    gold buddha clay buddha are all buddhas
    good man bad man are all men
    truth
    lies

are all formed of words, —real genius never reveals himself
photos are only phantoms

take photos to keep the image, record words to keep the
sound, read books to keep the mind
children do not study hard: stay down to keep up
golden sail on huge green waves
children's visual lunch

Hand-Copied Paperback   Nepal

ready for dinner, both hands on the map

choice goods: elastic bands are made of imported
three-splice
high power rubber bands and seven-colored soft satin
ordinary goods: elastic bands are made of imported
two-splice
rubber bands and soft satin and embroidery

not too tight

Hand-Copied Paperback   Vietnam

lurid, lurid botanical garden
a steamship passes by peels away half an orange
lurid, lurid orange peel
reveals plain style flesh, steamship, shipbow, in Hanoi
raging waves
botanical garden

Hand-Copied Paperback, rolling snowballs
little snowballs, big snowballs, little snowballs
little thaw, big thaw

water temperature lower than that of snow, clay urns
    filled with plum pollen
knowledge: a secret joy

3371   ......out of Shiguan China......(Analects · 30)
3372   ......+ that city wall + at that time......
3385   ......must be assailed......
3394   all these......
3414   ......+ the people ++......
3426   ......to no avail (Analects · four six)
3438   ......+ house its sun man (Yin · one two)
3476   ......gold (Yin · three)
3477
3519   ......down+++......
3553   have +......
3570   · three......
3571   · five......
3579   ......+ its place......
3580   ......+ the state......
4028   ......inner wall too (Analects · two five)
4486   ......eating fish...... (Six · one)
4488   ......as husband...... (Yin · four)
4489   ......+ take......
4548   ......+ yin yang
4557   ......+ ten......
4675   ......+ position......

陈东东
　　　祝雪的太阳

雪地上的玻璃片，冰层底下的圆形红石
把花开进屋子的白昼
它们都是你手上的枝条
是走出山谷的白色裸女面对着庭院
她河流一样柔韧的四肢
她的乳房
她丰满的臀和汇阴之上乌黑的一大片
它们都是你手上的枝条
是祝雪的太阳悬挂在枝上
如同画课后孩子的作业

她在你的院子里跳舞
她闪亮的锁骨
月亮一样晃动的足踝和唇舌之间芬芳的性
它们都是你手上的枝条
是红色圆石祝雪的太阳，孩子们闲来看云女
玻璃
这些荃杆摇成的花朵
雪地上的白昼和塑料鞋一样僵硬的冬天
它们都是你手上的枝条
是祝雪的太阳
冶去铺展照亮这个洁白的裸女

(1984)

Chen Dongdong
was born in Shanghai
in 1961. He is a 1984
graduate of Shanghai
Teachers' College,
and currently he
works in the resource
room of the Shanghai
Association of
Industry and
Commerce. His
poems have appeared
in a number of
literary magazines in
China, including
*New Observation,
China, Poetry,
Shanghai Literature,
Writers, Modern
Chinese Poetry,*
and *First Line.*

Snow-Covered Sun

Bits of broken glass on snowy ground,
frozen red stones,
on a white night the flowers that bloom indoors—
all these are branches in your hand.

Naked, she faces your yard from the valley,
arms soft as the river,
breasts, full buttocks, sweet belly, V stroke
of dark hair—
all these are branches in your hand.

The snow-covered sun
hangs on the trees
like a five-year old's watercolor.

In your yard she dances,
collarbones shining,
ankles shimmering like the moon,
scented sex between lips and tongue—
all these are branches in your hand.

The snow-covered sun
burns like a red stone,
like a glass children gaze through
at the clouds.

CHEN DONGDONG

Swaying petals,
white night on snowy ground
winter stiff as plastic sandals—
all these are branches in your hand.

The snow-covered sun
sheds its cold light
on her bare feet.

Finally

Fall's over.
My hands no longer open to the sun.
Fallen leaves on the streets,
silence in the garden square.
After the young women pass by,
someone remembers autumn.

In the hallway
or in the shadow of slogans:
A white light.
Who is that woman?
Who is it that has shattered the iceberg?

The bus runs like an iron bird,
a yellow songbird.
How I long to take a walk
above the bridge,
facing the sunny sky,
as in autumn.

失 遇

你是沿着河岸从我面前走去了
我说：远游的人！请你回头

你是回过头了，并且从我面前沿河走去了

你又从我面前沿河岸走去了
我说，远游的人！请你回头

你是回过头了，并且从我面前沿河走去了

91.6.28. 拉萨

He Zhong (also called Sarding Nuofu) is ethnically Yugu, Tibetan and Mongolian. He was born in 1963. Since 1985, he has lived in Tibet, where he now works as an editor of the magazine *Tibet Tours.* His poems and prose have appeared in various magazines in China. His book of poems, *The Last Good Wine,* is forthcoming from the Writers' Press. He is a member of the Chinese Writers Association.

The Vast Land

Because of a butterfly
I fall in love with all flowers
to experience reaching the throat
with my air-like antenna.

The wind always slips
behind time's back.

The vast land
melts into the silence of mountains
and the most vivid scene
is in the rough patterns of the rocks.

HE ZHONG

When We Walked into the City

When we walked into the city
it was pouring.

Like birds
all the pedestrians
hid under the trees on the sidewalks.

We passed through the streets
careless, our faces wet.

The bamboo chair under the roof
scared my thoughts away
with its anxious waiting.

The conspiracy of the evening
startled the withered wings of a rain swallow.

From the phoenix bush
we besieged the buildings.

You Come from Far Away

The slanting sun passes by.
Thin wind of the morning.
Stones bathed in colors
awaken tree leaves.
You come from far away,
a rose between your lips.

You come from far away.
The soft body of the soil
is freighted with yellow fruit.
Pigeons fly soundlessly over the temple roofs
wrapped in pine smoke.
Shepherds on the grass
gaze up.
The sound of bells fades.

The Cold Spirit of Snow

With its eyes fixed on the farthest goal
the horse crosses the valley.
Its tongue sticks out.
Only emptiness everywhere.

Who can stand still
in the place where eagles fly?
The stone gate you entered
is my exit.
The sun has never shone
on its top.

That strange bird
may never land here again.
What you desire
is a decoration for fables:
a pink baby,
smoke above a village,
a wide river.

Mountains and rivers excite you once more.
I'm thinking of my childhood bluebird,
the small windmill,
and the haystack—
My breath turned into
the cold spirit of snow.
How I wanted to see the ocean.

The Last Bottle of Good Wine

Don't forget the dreams I walked through:
the dark blue fire, the dancing songs
and the white horse that no one could stop
when it galloped across the red river.
Those ripples, those water flowers
are eternal images, the remaining glory of human history.
You, little boy, barefooted,
your torture still goes on
even after the water drops have punched a hole through the
rock.
Evil words travel all over the world.
I, left behind, with the last bottle of good wine for company
have dissolved helplessly
into a poem.

HE ZHONG

Missing the Encounter

You passed by me along the riverbank.
I said "Traveler, please look back!"

You looked back, and passed by me along the riverbank.

Again you passed by me along the riverbank.
I said "Traveler, please look back!"

You looked back, and passed by me along the riverbank.

Spring That Is Beyond Definition

These gods drift away from the snowy land.
Their swords wound the eyes staring at the dusk.
In the east giant lions
are crossing the mountain.

Another light comes through the cloud.
Another poppy flower blooms.
Light spreads at the end of the world,
a miracle hidden in my breast.

I'm blessed.
Everyone is blessed.
White clouds blossom like snow lotus,
the holy grail that steals the last days of the world.

High Land

Who dares to gaze at the lambs?

The eternal grassland, flowers everywhere,
children descending the mountain—
the sun embraces it all, but the clouds
are still lazy.

Children descend the mountain;
shall we continue our journey towards the east?

Certain periods, certain periods of time are
lifesaving, you depend on them
like depending on your own shadow—
I too want to descend the mountain
on the back of my horse, clouds
trailing behind us
like the loves I lost,
one after another.

The melancholy old shepherd, facing the mountains,
has not spoken a word.
After the tribes are dissolved,
and just as speechless, an eagle lands on the black cliff.

Under a Tree

Many days
I sit like this,
the blue emptiness
rubbing my forehead.
Dusk falls easily.
Along the road: two or three pedestrians.
Here and there the wind stirs up opaque ripples.
Leaves glint like gold coins.
Many days
I sit just like this.
Can't remember what should be done
or where to go.
Many days
are like this:
Facing the empty eye of my life
I daydream or sing.

Flowing Water

If you think it's water then it's water
and if it keeps moving it becomes time.
When we gaze with full attention
at a flower a cloud or a butterfly
we see how naturally
the water wets the flower the cloud
and the little belly of the butterfly.
If we think of how time flows
we'll realize
how we too can be dissolved
into a flower a cloud a butterfly
or a tree.

The Past Is a Cup from My People

The One-horned Tribal Chief

Lord Mang, I cannot follow
your strings
in blood, or in flesh.

The eagle has flown away, Lord Mang.
Your flower stands in the sky.
My hands reach out from the earth.
The sun flows like water.

Do Not Hurry

The gate opens, the flock pours out.
My love, do not hurry.
I'm a lamb
under your whip.
When the moon comes out, your song
will tear the evening's heart.

Come here. In the tent
your name appears on each page.
The last snowstorm is approaching the grassland.
Do you smell its untouchable fragrance?

The Past Is a Cup from My People

Through my clothing, children's songs.
Rusty wheels creak along.
Pluck your strings, master,

HE ZHONG

the past is a cup from my people
and the soil that buries our lives.

What holds you to the land?
Not the running horses that never look back.
It is your wine, the cup in your hand.
Brother, on such a fine night,
pluck your strings—
the past is tears in my people's eyes.

边缘

爸爸
我从不说谎
我受的教育
使我变成现在的模样

我不善于在白天
暴露我的身体和思想
我怕一些不知名的飞鸟
怕它们投下的阴影
砸在我光裸的背部
我必须敞开卧室的全部门窗
必须单发
或者自虐
我想让所受的教育
带我走出这边缘
爸爸
别人对我行为不端
我是否要告诉你

那闪烁而颤抖的小镜
布满夜晚
我要蒙蔽自己
再蒙蔽所有爱我恨我的人
这和我受的教育有关吗
别人在广场晒太阳
而我只能在夜里
让蜘蛛相互的对话
荒芜我的门槛

An artist and art
critic as well as a
poet, Jia Wei was
born in Yunnan, 1966.
She has been writing
poetry since 1990.

我看见大群的羊
从众人中走过
我不懂得管理它们
我只能把羊也当作是语言的动物
有意让它们穿越街市
爸爸
我想我难以厌倦那些火苗
如我愿意蒙蔽自己一样
把这些骚动的灰烬
当作黄金
空空如也的天空啊
尽善尽美的飞虫不知去向

我站立于此
观看那些落叶
我浑身沾满枯黄的气味
我作画或是写诗
都不能打消这特殊的气味
那是蜘蛛吗
一种浓妆的谋略的空中之物

我想我不该是现在的样子
我受的教育
使我变得像别人一般聪明
爸爸
你看见我在空地上站立
那些撒落我周身的树叶
是我所有的隐私
它们覆盖了我的脚趾
它们落在我的耳廓上
使我听不清
任何声音

Edge

Father,
I never tell lies.
My education
has made me what I am
though I should be living a different existence
enjoying home life
and bearing children for some man.

During the day
I'm not good at exposing
my body and my thoughts.
I'm afraid of unknown birds,
afraid of their shadows
clawing my naked back.
I must open all the bedroom windows,
must either become mean
or torture myself.
I hope my education
will lead me beyond this dangerous edge.
Should I tell you,
Father, about
someone's indecent behavior towards me?

I'm covered with
trembling dew.
I want to deceive myself,
deceive those who love or hate me.
Father,
I had a number of abortions with this man.
Does this have anything to do with my education?
People are sun bathing
but I can only eavesdrop

at the threshold
on the conversations of spiders.

I watch flocks of sheep
passing through crowds.
I don't know how to care for them—
You've never taught me.
I have no choice but to regard them
as animals that speak
and make them cross streets,
make them forget about
distant pastures.
Father,
I can't see through the dust,
and the restless flames
are as satisfying
as gold
or self-deception.
Oh, empty sky,
where are your perfect insects and birds?
I sit here in silence,
watching leaves fall that will never return.
I'm bathed in a stale smell,
Father,
and can't get rid of it
no matter how much I write or paint.

Is that a spider,
a cunning creature
in the air?
I should be what I am.
My education
has made me as clever as others.
I know I'm a terrible disappointment

to those who look at me
with love or hatred.

Father,
I was born into pain.
what should I do?
Why can't my work or ideas
change people's views?
With a smile,
my head crooked to one side,
I stand in an empty place
watching insects and birds.
I'm used to this moment.

Father,
look how the fragrance of the fields
has dampened my dry ear.

JIA WEI

Black Rails

The train is coming.
With my hands over my ears
I walk past its windows.

The black rails
lie on either side of my cheeks.
Their noise deafens me,
then zigzags into the distance.
Their cold arms
flail in the wind.
I stand to one side to let the train pass.

I walk onto the rails
and sit between them.
I look around—
not a single clean place
to lie down and make love.
When the train disappears
my fingers are numb with anxiety.
The clouds.
My trusting face
smudged by the dark smoke.

I lie down,
letting the train grind over my rails.
I look up at the sky.
Smoke smudges
my trampled cheeks again.

Scene A

It's not yet two in the afternoon.
Flying away from the window
a bird leaves droppings.
The sun is dazzling.
My dog can't keep her eyes open
so I send her to bed.

Who's found me here?
I hate this knocking in the afternoon.
My dog wakes up
barking.
I don't get to the door
until the shadow of the intruder outside
has disappeared.
I hear he's a bastard
and I'm from a high-class family.
He's not worth going out with.
I reach out of the window
to clean up the bird shit.
Thinking about napping in the chair.
I've seen all kinds of people
especially women
but I still wonder what makes us so
much alike or different.
My fingers touch something
suspicious.

I should have answered the door.
If other women can do it
so can I,
and even better.

Jia Wei

It's almost four.
I've been sitting here two hours,
the chair squeaking under my weight
and the weight of my loneliness.
My dog has waked up.
The bird that flew away at two
has returned.
Well, I'm not sure it's the same one
but on my window sill
there are more droppings.

Liang Xiaoming was born in Hangzhou in 1963. At the age of five he went to the countryside with his father to do manual labor and didn't return to Hangzhou until 1982. In 1981, he read Whitman's *Leaves of Grass* and was inspired to begin writing poetry. Presently he works at the Hangzhou Youth Center.

Individual

You and I raise our mugs
and drink our tea.
We smile at each other
and nod elegantly.
We're fastidious.
We talk about business,
study our fingers,
and express our opinions.
Finally
we walk our separate ways.

At the gate we shake hands
and look into each other's eyes.
When we descend the stairs
I wave at you
if you're ahead of me
and say "come again"
Or if I'm the first
you wave at me
and say "walk slowly"

Then we flee
in different directions,
and if it's raining
we have our raincoats.

Since the Creation of Words

Since the creation of words
what fun have I had?
I look for news of the sun
like a swallow's tail.
I came into this world
with spring and rain.
What fun have I had?
Flowers bloom on my head
like a pumpkin song.
At the table where people gather
I watch the dusk
being murdered by ants.
A banana life is peeled by fingers.
All roads lead to the kitchen.
The only moon
is the love that rose yesterday.

Alone,
with four pocketfuls of lovely emotions,
I came to earth
and was rejected at the threshold.
What fun have I had?
I dance with grass in the wind
and play a tree bark harmonica for the stars
under the narrow skylight.

I read a book
about a coup in Latin America,
a line of polished boots
marching on sunny streets.
A tear
hangs in my eye.
Time tumbles and flies from my hand.
What fun have I had?

Permission

Bleed me with the knife,
drain the pus. My crops,
my white-haired grandma, singing.

I burn my flesh, the flame laps,
scorches my plump earlobes.
I'm on fire, everyone is on fire.
I'm in pain, it is the pain of humanity.

I love this street and this small room.
For this love, I'll start talking.
For this love, I'll start dying today.

刘漫流

继续让我寻找一种语言

在海上　面对海　烈士们已经奋起
为了维护至高无上的荣誉

我不会忘记这个年代　我不会忘记这个地点
艰难的夜晚　被篡改的航海日志

那不断地泛滥在头顶的水泥
正在重新凝结的岩石　作为见证的岩石

也沦落了黑暗　我隐居的深水
漩涡的位置

那顺着脸颊一起滴落的泪水和石块
我的同类　我的城市

需要飞鸟的协作才能完成的浩大工程
囚禁在海上的人们　联合起来

越过那早已成为局限的天空
解放我们自己

Liu Manliu is the pen name of Liu Yojun. Born in Shanghai in 1962, he graduated from Huadong Teachers' College, and now teaches at a medical college in Shanghai. With Meng Lang and Mo Mo he is a co-founder of the poetry journals *On the Sea* and *The Continental*. He is also an editor of the magazine *Modern Chinese Poetry*.

Mayfly's Journal

Poetry aches and freezes.
Melancholy narrator below the waterline,
foam's masterpiece,

I turn my back on the memories,
the dangerous fish in the distance,

days in dark seclusion,
oblivious to the grinding of fish teeth.

They can't hear the bad news
about my vanished poet-brothers.

Water, gigantic
curves, dizzying.

Who will notice the body's double trembling,
breathing like a thread, like an ant.

Finally, born in shame, the first pair of wings.
Another pair!

Lightly I shake my wings
and take off,

writing my name on the surface of the water,
tremendous dream under a lotus leaf's shadow.

I pass over the land
and the market of cattails

like an insect kindergarten
or the grand ball of the white lotus.

I accept the beautiful scenes along the shore
as a consolation.

First trip without the help of a machine
into a multiple world.

The thread on my tail
is there to maintain balance.

In my own sky
I rocket into tragedy.

A crash site
teaches the newcomers.

To begin like an apprentice,
to summarize like an expert.

Unconsciously I'm approaching eternity,
nearing multiplicity.

Oh humans, why are you so greedy?
Give me a day.

One day is enough.
Give me one day of eternity.

No need to get excited about beginning or end:
Measure does not exist.

Death is only the ritual
of leaving your life.

At twilight we fly in groups,
facing sunset together.

Circles inside circles,
the first and last days of a lunar month merely secondary.

A soul that is multiple enough
can hold anything.

No need to point at the sky and say
"This is a second"

or "a billion light years":
The explosion is ongoing,

the cosmos in a moment,
all of us existing in this one fantastic shot, dancing.

Flying, too, is a performance,
but without an audience.

It is the ultimate affirmation,
proof that we deserve to be noticed.

To fly is to embrace this attitude,
to embrace the land and its inhabitants.

The sea. Pity for a grain of salt.
Our flight is without limits.

We live our lives as you take vacations—
in one day we mate, lay eggs, and die.

Liu Manliu

Autograph Book

Title page—like daytime before I was born, light at
    the other end of the tunnel.
In a blind navel I found a white fear.

A baby grown accustomed to the dark is impressed
by its first look at the light.

To praise darkness, to sing about the dark, is a habit
I've cultivated in the core of the sea.

I'm as mysterious as a sea urchin, as distant as a fish,
and I cry like a mermaid,
each drop of my tears the size of a shell.

The colors on my forehead interweave,
recording the ocean's tremor:
The shrinking skull is a book of poetry.

I haven't forgotten to write down my name and the date.

The first page—in the center of a small, dark universe,
I'm warm and safe, surrounded by amniotic memory.

A universe in a shell—sometimes out of necessity it hides.
I suck in the delicious liquid of darkness.
My hands tear history.

The worst crime is a pearl,
its pale core a grain of salt,
and most pearls are discolored.

From one to two is not just a turning of the page.
The sea is the source. For me, there's always
another eye, open at the bottom of the brain.

Now I understand your language.

On the floor of the sea I suffered the heaviest blow,
which taught me life.

In the electric chair of the universe, the contractions became
    violent.

Some misfortune is inescapable,
some birthmarks indelible.

The design that comes between the third and fourth
    pages is the native tongue
        that not even the sea can wash away.

At the moment of flight, you say I need light,
and the light shines on you,
and a tall god is blurred by a halo.

Thus religion was born and nurses became angels.

All the angels are white dwarf stars.
All the crows are fallen angels.

Like fixed stars and their moons, nights are the
    collapse of daytime.

We've been forcing ourselves to believe
that a thousand years of darkness will be rewarded
with a thousand years of happiness.

Contractions made me forget my last name on Page X—
the whitest page, the criminal page,
where the light suddenly switches on and off,
and the wounded one is comforted.

I turned this page, but forgot to number it.
Deliberately, I didn't darken it.

As for you, when you open your eyes
you'll see the light. and then go blind again.

It's time to utter your first words
in a language that can be understood throughout the world.

Don't let this X turn into a swastika.
Don't be sentenced before you sing.

My only concern is the force-field of language.

An untimely end is like the night before I was born,
like a white moth turned black, turned into a
        dance or a mutation.

Suddenly I grew into a singer and my first song
        was dedicated to night,

to the first and last night, to all the living and the dead,
the pattern of the trembling sea, in which a youth drowned.

He taught me how to shout and drink
—sunlight or blood—at the same time:
sunlight in the dark, blood in the light,
and how to see light in the dark, and by that light to read my
        own handwriting.

Time. Space.

As I Search for a Language

Before the sea, on the sea, martyrs rose
to defend their honor.

I'll never forget
the night the ship ran aground.

Cement splashed on our heads
and poured over the bystander rocks.

Darkness enveloped us, then deep water and a whirlpool.
I lived there in seclusion.

Tears and stones ran down my cheeks:
my companions, my city.

This vast undertaking needs birds.
Prisoners of the sea, unite.

We'll cross the limits of sky
and free ourselves.

On seashores, we'll gather twigs and stones
to open up new lands.

We'll sharpen metal and words
to launch at the sea froth.

The speared fish is proto-human
and the singing ocean spits white foam.

Blood all over my body, my chest tattooed with words.
Magnificent images flash on the wave crests.

Liu Manliu

I obey time and the flowing waters,
strolling along every shore of the world.

Tides fall and rise. In the robe of my ancestors, under
the same moon,
I write and read poetry.

On the front and sleeves, on the shoulders and sides,
angry miracles whirl without end.

Patterns already deeply chiseled in the waves
engrave themselves on the cliffs and the shoreline.

We discuss hog-tied art, tattooed art.
A language rebellious and free

floods our enclave,
leaving its sweat on every shell.

Our words are wet with sparkling stars
like red songs sung to a moon above the sea.

How we treasure our mother tongue
and scrutinize the language of diplomacy!

Settling into pedestrian rhythm,
we live in a microcosm, part of an international poetry clique.

And remember this lesson:
Publication equals betrayal!

An armed uprising
was aborted because we were so green in battle.

84

Polluted by blood and vomit,
with shadows on its lungs,

the whole sea gets cramps
like the leg of a drowning swimmer.

Language gasps.
The air fills with distilled mercury.

It's an age measured by metal,
sunk in roots.

Golden years wasted!
Time to cry out:

Let me search for a language
in the dark, in the face of the dark.

Liu Manliu

To Poets

1

Flooded with stubborn sleep.
Sliding roofs. At midnight, an empty flagpole.
Birds fly.

Flames leap on a polluted sea.
The smell of asphalt.
Unburied corpses. And writing.

All the endangered riches, commanding me to write. And
to write with water.

2

Since you accept the purity of knowledge and believe
that publishing is corruption,
you are doomed to darkness, doomed to write with
buried words.

The stars have not been differentiated for you.
They are pagan signatures on the ceiling.

Fall is voluptuous, white eggs under black wings,
a vast lonely center of words.

And night is voluptuous, the blank texts hermetic—
Rub them and all you get is static.

So many fountains languish in meditation.

3

To sing in the morning and play an empty tune.
To mine bright-colored minerals,
to study their substance and smell.
Old iron in the shape of fire.
A rescued tongue in a deep throat.
Dust stirred by breathing.
In floating wells, words speak and listen.

Coming from different professions, aliens cross the border
under the moon
to gather in a print shop.
With coal and captive pencils,
they summon language
to join their lonely panning for gold,
to seek the constant meaning of work.

How simple and serious this operation!
In the sacred factory
we learn the craft of struggle and creation.
Every night under the tyranny of white paper,
we preserve images that mean something
and remember haggard times.

4

Brilliant speeches, vicious jokes, and grammars
    that revise dreams.
Faulty expressions in a poem, dramatic soliloquies,
and the rhythms of planets rotating.
Vocabularies of schizophrenia, the slogans of demonstrators,
the telephone operator's pidgin English. Slips of the tongue.

The negations, the diplomatic innuendoes,
the national hearsay and the quibbling of official
    spokespersons.
Expert jargons, civic propaganda, and the secret
    gestures of hermits.
The local customs of multinational corporations.

The animal names that the master shouts into his
    apprentice's ear
and the dirty words of angry washerwomen.
A sow in heat at the butcher store and a donkey penis
    dangling in a restaurant window.

The friction of forced mating, stains on jockey shorts
    drying on a porch.
The suffocation of a first kiss. Lost alphabets. Exercises
    for correcting a stutter.

All the nicknames for a crucifix. An epoch
    of language abandoned.
Aphasia on meeting an old friend.
Ceremonial prayers, classic texts chiseled in granite.

5

Ah! The glorious saga, the staggering steps of elders.
The deep plowing of ancestors.
The silver handwriting of their journey.

Degenerated royal descendants of the ocean.
Lazy, primitive finned creatures.
Coral reefs growing on predecessors' corpses.
Wrecked ships and the snowy storms of silver fish.

Fighting fish, crayon fish,
baby angel fish, the dazzling ads on their bodies
and the fishermen's expression as they tighten their nets.

The goods and the tides in the mercantile night.
Seafood sales.
Goldfish and lava as perfect as pictures
under the crushing rule of rare metal.

From heaven to hell,
a series of grand tableaux.
Innumerable civilizations lost.

The blood of soldiers in the World Wars.
Diseases and darkness in the depths of civilization.
Even the naked beach is infected.

The sea that in its fever used to overflow
has left this single trace:
a grain of salt at the corner of a poet's mouth.

The topography of my home and rivers
is invisible on official maps.

I must remain here to the end,
ready to go down with my land!

6

March to our ultimate downfall! The way food
    decays in summer.
At the end of the banquet table, we are spat-out bones.
Silverware for the sun.

A pond gleams. The drowned still cling
to night's peaceful air.

We sit around white marble, waiting for miracles.
    Water responds.
Poisoned air vomits up strange animals and plants.
They grow, leap and die, savoring color, odor, life.

We've sunk so low! So low!
Living our lives in the posture of struggle.

7

Coral is stronger,
more stubborn, with a complicated family life
and entangled branches.

Stairways lead us
up or down
to pick the fruit of day and the fruit of night.

In a center unreachable by language
God's finger rests.
The sculptor's eye
perfects the fruit,
preserves the core of sadness.

Hand in hand, rose to rose,
giving life,
cultivating death.
Who can believe
we touch the same light?

In the splintered mirror
the sun reflects different wounds
and leaves only
a warm orange light.

8

One taste and you'll know that famine is harvest.
You'll turn to the dark and cultivate groves of passion fruit.

With diamonds for seeds
they brighten the night, glowing with sparks of rebellion.

Fall is voluptuous, the waste land extends to my pillow.
Paper and a sweater are prepared for you.
Night is deep. Return to imagination. Return to generosity.
Guard the treasure in our hearts.

The sun begins its summary.

9

Diseases are spread on a stained flytrap.
A plane crosses the night.
The cruel century spins its black propeller.

Birds, in and out of focus. Priests
wander through the sky.
Smiling souls.

Five thousand million souls.
My ancestors and descendants
command me to write these words in blood.

流亡者箴言

孟浪

就住在自己的家里
就住在自己的心里
宣布我自己的流放。

世界，我已走过了你的终点
世界，你还有什么漫长可以让我跨越？

就活在自己的家里，粮田里
就活在自己的心里，果园里
就活在我的流放里。

世界，我已带走了你的起源，
世界，你必须接受来自我的创造或毁灭。

粮田里，我睡着了
果园里，我在梦中站起身修剪枝叶。

就在自己的家里，到处是新谷
就在自己的心里，堆满了水果
世界，请贡献更多送远！

1990.5.24.

Meng Lang is the
pen name of Meng
Juliang, born in
Shanghai in 1961,
and a graduate of
the Shanghai
Machinery Institute.
He is the author of
*A Survivor of the
Century* (Li River
Publishing, 1988);
and co-editor of *A
Panorama of Chinese
Modern Poetry
Groups 1986-1988*
(Tongji University
Press). With Liu
Manliu and Mo Mo
he is a co-founder
of the poetry journals
On the Sea and *The
Continental.* He lives
in Shanghai.

Exile Admonition

I want only to live in my own house.
I want only to live in my own mind.
I announce this as my own exile.

World, I've traversed your boundaries.
Do you have anything else for me to cross?

I want only to live in my house, among my rice fields.
I want only to live in my mind, my orchard.
I want only to live out my exile.

World, I've grasped your origin.
Now you must grasp my origin and my annihilation.

In the open fields, I fall asleep.
In the orchard, I dream of getting up to cut the trees.

In my own house, new rice overflows.
In my own mind, fruit lies heaped.
O world, give me more distance!

This Age Has TB

Our epoch is sick:
wracked with diseases, my body shadows it.

I'm coughing.
My lungs are sick with love.

I'm attacked repeatedly,
I'm getting it so often, so loudly.

It's a sick time: I want to love more,
but my health gets worse.

Violent coughing shakes me.
I'd love to shout, but I've lost my voice.

A World

As your fist slips open, a world falls apart.
You have to grab it by the collar,
treat it like a human being
hungry for a blood transfusion.

You have to locate the wound,
remove its underwear,
give it a free hand.

For years this world has been in a coma,
leaning on your shoulder.
This is your only chance to save it.

Settling

After a loss
the body
is stripped.

The traveler's toothbrush
demonstrates eternity
day by day.

All meaning
is reduced to a faded flower
and a plane crash.

Refugees pour onto another island
to see the rotten fish—
a skeleton trapped in the wreckage.

The dinosaurs suffered a much earlier defeat.
Now they live in the cities,
their faces anonymous in crowds.

年轻的预言者

年轻的预言者是他造就了
一座留下旷野的房屋
被雪涌上他的头
现在雪忍住的只是泪水

让冷风吹落的树十分纷纷
挺身于窗小
四季的尖顶滑落
他如实地看到黑暗看到光

大地的核心
在午夜的江湖中萌动
蜂巢屋檐连缕白烟
山的影子不在山上

被蛇磨光的洞口
把他引上缓慢的深渊
命运在陷落
像刀柄一样敲打

催促大地的呼吸在敲打
猛烈的冰块冲下铁间
过河的人想不通
太麻痹了这个世界

园子里没有打开的灌木
依旧保存了自缢的痕迹
死亡先声夺人
谁的脚步还风在天空悠荡

《洞与物 (1989-1991)》
第二卷 第一篇

Born in Beijing in 1961, Mo Fei went into exile with his family in the Taihang Mountains of Hebei Province, when the Cultural Revolution began in 1966, returning 13 years later to Beijing, where he graduated from the Beijing Teachers' College. His poems have appeared in the magazines *Poetry, People's Literature, October,* and *First Line.* Collections of his poems include *Palm Tree* (1982), *Maniac's Paradise* (1985), and *Blank Space in a Gap* (1987), all published in mimeograph. His recent work includes *The Century's Twilight,* a book-length poem (10,000 lines) and *Words and Objects,* a sequence of 272 poems. He lives in Beijing.

From *Words and Objects*

Prelude

In that place either silent or blind
you're writing the only poem.
In the backyard of time
you've written lines to replace words and objects.

You have started
the poem that has no beginning,
that no one can kidnap.
It's almost winter.
The nib of the pen gleams.
The last stroke in the dark
brings the world to a sudden halt.

Those whose ears were stolen
will never forgive.
The disaster caused by the snowstorm
woke up all the drunkards.

A gardener tends death and roses
to learn wisdom
within the short span of his life.
Doors and windows tightly closed,
how you wish you could keep your relatives here
and let trees enjoy the stillness of twilight.

You're doomed
to write this sole poem.
Words are short of breath,
but you linger on.

MO FEI

The Sound of Chopping Wood

The sound of chopping wood—
crisp, penetrating.
It has nothing to do
with time.

The gardener's hands,
like the wood, have nowhere to go.
Morning to night
he's haunted by pain.

Dimly
memory opens a crack
in a walnut tree.
When he thinks about it,
afternoon is really the most difficult time.
The gardener has a tender spot in his heart.
The logs for winter
are piled in the deepest corner of the season
higher than the flames.

Outside the window snow falls,
justice grows.
Death threatens the limits of language.
Everything flourishes,
flowers never fade,
and trees don't need names
to live.

How accurate the sound of chopping wood,
and how resolute!
Even the gardener can't believe
that he's so sure of himself.

Stuck in Place

The person stuck in this room
is scared of the table.
Words are an infinity of holes
he doesn't know how to repair.

A piece of blank paper lives a cleaner life.
Everything is a habit.
He often wonders about the clock on the wall.
If it would only stop ticking, it might be more accurate.

A premonition throbs in his temples.
He can hear nothing.
Thunder stuns the woods
as in a vicious dream.

Dawn arrives
after a sleepless night.
An utterly unjust fire
saves his life from the book.

MO FEI

Coins Flung in Four Directions

Coins flung in four directions
and the sky clear as a curse.
You recognize what it means
to forget the things behind the words.

The missionary exiles himself
in order to alter time.
The heavy leaves of the plane trees
overstate the weight of the rain.

Keep tumbling from sleep.
Jump for joy to the top of a bush.
Worry about the coming night
as if you were fleeing other people's lives.

A perfect lesson, ruined,
but you can't forget her.
On both sides of your head hang ignorant ears.
You are still indifferent, still quiet.

Young Prophet

The young prophet built
a house in the wilderness.
Snow gusting above his head,
he had to hold back more than tears.

Let the bushes awaken in the cold wind
and vanish in the bonfire.
When dust fell from the towers of the four seasons
he saw the dark and the light as they were.

The core of the earth
sprouted into the vastness of midnight.
White smoke rose from beehives.
The shadow of the mountain split in two.

A cave shiny with snakes
led into an abyss
where fate
trembled like a knife.

The earth shook.
Icebergs rushed through the gates.
Travelers couldn't understand
why the world was so violent.

There were no bushes in the garden.
Only an effigy was preserved.
Death made the first gesture.
Whose footsteps floated in the sky?

Mo Fei

This Is Not the Last

I'm not the last
person to be punished by language.
The new wooden house
gets knocked down by a tree.

The prisoner
sets traps around himself.
If he escapes alive,
he'll take his crimes with him.

He has no other shortcut.
A knife blade separates life and death.
Light is cut open
and bent by the lonely sky.

The world is painful as fate.
Words are shackles.
Once he's learned how to confess
no one can ever defend him.

又 馋 又 饿

馋了想尝尝怨女内闹闹凤凰的熟香

饿了想吃点冰川喝点阳光

我讨厌大心平的姑娘

讨厌带看画铁城手表

研究井冈山野菜营养价值的大学生

我好不容易学会忠诚

却发现世界早已背叛我

老惹着愤怒

所以我开口大笑不好看

咪咪笑才好看

为了保卫蓝天我赶走了所有的乌云

为了保卫篝火我点燃了所有的荒屁

为了保卫秋天我把自己结成果实

馋了饿了我想吃一切

快闭上眼睛看着我又馋又饿的样子我多不好意思呀

Mo Mo, born in Shanghai in 1964, has been writing poetry since he was fifteen. His books include *The Skinny Teenage Boy of the Nation, The Fossil of the Depressed X and Y, The Big Chaos,* and *In the Darkness.* Publication of his long poem "Growing up in China" led to his arrest in 1986; he was arrested again in 1992. He has completed two novels: *Our China Dream* and *Homeless.* He is co-founder of three poetry journals: *On the Sea* and *The Continental,* with Meng Lang and Liu Manliu, and *Modern Chinese Poetry,* with Mang Ke and Tang Xiaodu.

Betrayal

At night I reach out my hands,
the bright fingers gesturing
in the direction of the roses, my head bent silently
toward their blooming, the withered
soft fingers gesturing now
in the direction of
the waves, my head bent silently
toward their calm,
the cold fingers gesturing now
in the direction of the cliff, my head bent silently
toward those who remain.
I slip into spring water, pebbles, cloves;
my hair has grown like wheat, but can't be harvested.

At night I reach out my hands,
the rough fingers gesturing
in the direction of language, my head bent silently
toward the talking, listening
slim fingers, gesturing
in the direction of a dream, my head bent silently
toward the beautiful scenes and nightmares.
At night I dream I'm thrown into a slaughterhouse,
death not a secret but a gaze.

Mo Mo

At dawn the fingers still gesture
in the direction of a song I once sang,
but now I've lost my voice.
The sun has risen and the firm gesturing
is in the direction of my motherland.
She gave birth to me, but now I am drifting farther away,
the sun blinds my eyes, the trembling fingers
gesture
in the direction of a city
which is holding a funeral for me
as if I were a puppet
not alive until touched by a hand.

Tears on my face, I can't see
where the last finger is gesturing.

If it's gesturing
in the direction of my imagination,
then it's gesturing
in the direction of time,
which is also at you.
When someone says the water is flowing fast,
you come over and make a whirlpool
to drown me, to choke me.
Then suddenly you point your finger
at the void.

Gluttonous and Hungry

When I'm famished, I want to taste dinosaur meat and smell
    the cooked phoenix.
When I'm starved, I want to eat icebergs and drink sunlight.
I hate girls with big front teeth,
hate the college students who study the nutritive value
of Jin Gangshan herbs with Citizen watches on their wrists.
Just when I've managed to learn how to be honest,
I discover the world has already betrayed me.
I'm bursting with anger.
That makes me look ugly when I laugh.
So instead I grimace.
To defend the blue sky, I drive away all the clouds.
To defend the bonfire, I set all the grasslands ablaze.
To defend autumn, I turn myself into fruit.
I want to devour everything in sight.
Quick, close your eyes!
It's embarrassing to be so hungry.

Mo Mo

Sold Out

Following my inclinations,
I sell dreams, cheap,
like a dog who has sold his master.
I sell epochs,
my body crosshatched with scars.
Diarrhetic and penniless as fresh air,
I sell time.
I sell country—motherland disappears.
I sell space—earth vanishes.
Holding the universe in my hand, I write you a love letter.

I sell holidays, along with loneliness.
Ignorant of the world
I sell everything:
life, breath, death.
But tonight you must listen.
I'm going to kiss you seriously
and turn over like a sunken boat—
You're the ocean,
the only thing I have left.

黑 夜

我的眼睛不由自主地流在黑夜

流在黑夜使我无家可归

在一比诉黑之中我成为夜游之神

夜雾中的光环蜂涌而至

那丰富而含混的色彩使我心领神会

所有色彩归宿于黑夜相安无事

游夜之神是凄惶的尤物

长着有肉垫的猫脚和蛇的躯体

怀着鬼鬼祟祟的兴趣回避着鸡叫

我到底想干什么

我走进庞大的夜

我是想把自己变成有血有肉的影子

我是想似睡似醒地在一切影子里玩游

真是个尤物是个尤物是个尤物

我似乎披着黑纱编起夜风

我是这样潇洒 轻松 飘飘荡荡

在夜晚一切都会成为虚幻的影子

甚至皮肤血肉和骨骼都是黑色

莫名其妙莫名其妙莫名其妙

天空和大海的影子也是黑夜

唐亚平

1985年10月 贵阳

Born in Sichuan in 1962, Tang Yaping received her bachelor's degree in philosophy from Sichuan University in 1983. She works as a journalist for Guizhou Province's television station. Her books of poetry include *Primitive Moon* (Guizhou People's Press) and *Moon's Expression* (Shenyang Press). She is a member of the Guizhou Writers Association.

Just Call Me by My Nickname

Just call me by my nickname
as you used to—
at home or in public
call me Qiao'r,
Crafty Girl, and I'll always
think of you as Qingwa,
my Diligent Boy, my Frog.
In the end these names
given by the land are best.
When it's time to plant,
call me your Seedling,
and when the grapes are ripe,
I'll be your Green Vine.
I'll call you Pomegranate Tree
when it rains,
and White Poplar when the wind blows.

These names have emerged from the soil.
Coming to us from the past,
from the fields, they are ours,
reaching back
to Taro's father and Black Ox's grandfather.
Qingwa, my Frog, my Diligent Boy,
give these gifts from the fields
to our sons and daughters,
and the land will yield greater names.

Black Night

Brothers and sisters, I may be transparent and penniless,
but trust my maturity.
Overnight my road has become a precipice.
I've decided to stand with my back to the sun
and let the shadow obscure my future.
Now you come toward me, calling me.
The echo falls like a pebble into the dry riverbed.
Brothers and sisters, where shall we go?
Transparency is all I have.
Trust my maturity.
Looking at you, I grow as old as the night.
To gain self-respect I choose silence in the dark.
No need to test my abyss with your kindness.
I'm beyond any conflict about my precipice.
I have accepted solitude and sorrow.
Brothers and sisters,
my heaviness surpasses all.

沉甸甸的，黑，比夜还黑，
比一个暴君还要镇压。
以看到黑暗中的炼钢厂，火
光亮了一个世纪
在六月呼啸而来，铁的力量
压倒一切。
铁，岩石之父，还是
来自黑人性格中的某种东西
黑暗
而盲目：它在那里
无需视的言词，与更为大的
元素之间，它是一个否定
但比肯定还要
肯定：它是铁，是坚定无言
不可被改为
法。

Wang Jiaxin was born
in 1957 in Hubei
Province, and
graduated from the
Chinese Department
of Wuhan University.
His major
publications are
Selected Poems, 1984
(Xian Press),
*Commemoration:
Selected Poems*
(Changjiang Publish-
ing, Wuhan, 1985),
*The Voice of
a Palm: Selected
Poems,* (Lijiang
Publishing, Guangxi),
and *The Encounter
of Man with the
World:* (Culture and
Arts Press, Beijing
1989). His recent
work has appeared
in the magazines
*People's Literature,
Changjiang
Literature, Today,*
and *First Line.*
Currently, he lives
in England.

Iron

Heavier than night, darker than dark,
cooler than the mind of a tyrant.
And the fire of the ironworks
torments a whole century.

The force of iron
overwhelms everything.

Iron, father of the rock,
is part of our nature.

Dark and blind,
it is there
between the words presented
and the greater nothingness: a negation,
yet more affirmative
than affirmation—Iron can't be
defeated, disputed, destroyed.

WANG JIAXIN

Words

Words
can penetrate objects like knives,
can rust,
can get blunt.

Knives enter
at a precise time and place,
stratum by stratum.

Words appear
in sinister light.
Sharp, bright, irrevocable,
they come from purgatory.

When the knives hit,
something unseen occurs,
and we tremble at its touch.

Railway Station

The abandoned station
retains the sounds
of the train that has left,
the wheels moving away, the rails rusting slowly....

Death crashed into this place,
Life so thirsty that each car

fiercely challenged the others
to a duel with real bullets.

One after the other, verbs disappear
like the centuries, and heaps of nouns
just lie among the adjective weeds
growing wild
between the rails....

WANG PING

没头没脑（节选）　　　王屏

肯尼迪机场…投奔发拉盏…没头没脑…什么…二十五美分
个电话…不…全部家当一只箱子一本词典二十五美元…地下室…
辗转反侧…美国梦消化不良…忍不住尖叫…不…担保人
就在楼上…静々的纽约之夜…凝视空间…没头没脑…
徬徨于清醒失落之间…又一夜…第一手肮钱抵扎票房租…
中国古董店…第五大道…秋叶落满流浪汉的衣衫…落满金色
的招牌…"两个世界"…皮萨饼车主…老板请客…第一次品尝
起士…太多的第一次…吐海老板的鞋袜…上不了柜面…没有
值观念…没生意细胞…太倔太傲做不了资本家的走狗…
出了店…出了地下室…寻找工作…两家饭馆…用来发拉盏…
用日中城…晚上读书…贝里治第一间住房…每月$180…四小
时地铁…读《尤利西斯》…或打盹…车身摇晃似摇篮…
似母亲的摇椅…上课时睡觉…时不念莎士比亚…不修荷学分就
得滚出美国…遍地黄金的纽约…浮尸进头在时代广场地铁…

Wang Ping, born in Shanghai, graduated from Beijing University in 1984, came to New York in 1985. Her books include *American Visa* (short stories), *Foreign Devil* (a novel), and *Of Flesh and Spirit* (poetry) from Coffee House Press. She is the recipient of poetry grants from the National Endowment for the Arts and the New York Foundation for the Arts, and a translation grant for this collection from the New York State Council on the Arts.

Syntax

She walks to a table
She walk to table

She is walking to a table
She walk to table now

What difference does it make
What difference it make

In Nature, no completeness
No sentence really complete thought

Language, like beast,
Look best when free, undressed

Of Flesh and Spirit

I was a virgin till twenty-three, then always had more than one lover at the same time—all secret.

In China, people go to jail for watching porno videos while condoms and pills are given out free.

When I saw the first bra my mom made for me, I screamed and ran away in shame.

For a thousand years, women's bound feet were the most beautiful and erotic objects for Chinese. Tits and asses were nothing compared to a pair of three-inch "golden lotuses." They must have been crazy or had problems with their noses. My grandma's feet, wrapped day and night in layers of bandages, smelled like rotten fish.

The asshole in Chinese: the eye of the fart.

A twenty-five-year-old single woman worries her parents. A twenty-eight-year-old single woman worries her friends and colleagues. A thirty-year-old single woman worries her bosses. A thirty-five-year-old woman is pitied and treated as a sexual pervert.

The most powerful curse: fuck your mother, fuck your grandmother, fuck your great-grandmother of eighteen generations.

One day, my father asked my mother if our young rooster was mature enough to jump, meaning to "mate." I cut in before my mother answered: "Yes, I saw him jump onto the roof of the chicken coop." I was ten years old.

Women call menstruation "the old ghost," science books call it "the moon period," and refined people say "the moonlight is flooding the ditch."

My first lover vowed to marry me in America after he took my virginity. He had two kids and an uneducated wife, and dared not ask the police for a divorce. He took me to see his American Chinese cousin who was staying in the Beijing Hotel and tried to persuade his cousin to sponsor him to come to New York. But his cousin sponsored me instead. That's how I'm here and why he went back to his wife, still cursing me.

Chinese peasants call their wives: that one in my house; old Chinese intellectuals: the doll in a golden house; in socialist China, husbands and wives call each other "my lover."

The story my grandma never tired of telling was about a man who was punished for his greed and had to walk around with a penis hanging from his forehead.

We don't say "fall in love," but "talk love."

When I left home, my father told me: "never talk love before you're twenty-five years old." I waited till twenty-three. Well, my first lover was a married coward. My first marriage lasted a week. My husband slept with me once, and I never saw him again.

WANG PING

Crossing Essex

River under clouds.
Mountains in the distance.

Crossing Essex
arm in arm
two teenage girls
lips half open
deep in their pink dreams.
A white-haired baby
stumbles toward his hapless mother.
An old man freezes in the middle of traffic.
No one listens to the sun.
No one follows the river.
The light turns red.

River of yellow cabs.

The first woman and man
jumped off Nuwa's hand.
Repaired heavens.
Ten thousand years of sleep.
Sitting by the river she smiled at her last mission.

They waded into the water.
Shadows sank to the bottom.

Earth burnt off the last rays.
Their bodies turned into maps.

The river is no obstacle.

The young Jews walk whispering past Wong's Kodak Express.
Their beards float,
their pants slip below their belly buttons.
Through his window of cosmetics
the old man winks at the teenagers.
Women chatter at Guss Pickles.
The sweet and sour smell drifts
toward the Williamsburg Bridge.
Underneath a man stares at his broken bottle of coconut milk
oozing into the subway grill.
A bee buzzes around the huge bare waist of the homeless
man.
I suddenly understand why Ted Berrigan took speed.

WANG PING

No Sense of Direction

So just like this   out of the plane at Kennedy   Destination
Flushing address   no sense of direction   what?   a quarter
for the pay phone   no   all her luggage   Twenty-five dollars
and a dictionary   first night in basement   sleepless   indi-
gestion of dreams   want to scream but no   her sponsor
upstairs   silent night   staring into space   no sense of direc-
tion   hover between awareness and loss   first month work-
ing to pay off the plane ticket   selling Chinese antiques
Fifth Avenue   leaves falling on the homeless blanket   on
the golden canopy of the store   "Two Worlds"   Pizza for
lunch   on the boss   first bite of cheese   throwing up on
the boss' shoes   no sense of value   no brain for business
too stubborn to be a running dog   out of the store   out of
the basement   out hunting for jobs   two restaurants
Flushing for weekend   midtown from Monday to Friday
first apartment room in Bay Ridge $180 for rent   four
hours underground   reading Ulysses in train   or dozing
rocking like a cradle   mother rocker   sleeping in class
sorry Shakespeare   tender mercies   full time school or get
out of America   lost in Times Square   "Someone give me a
quarter please"   no sense of direction   Malaysian Chinese
landlady   dream of becoming a fashion designer   furious at
the question if she was lonely   kicked out the next week
$250 a room at Elmhurst from a Taiwanese couple   can't
afford it   divorced engineer offers to pay half   offers to take
her to the Jersey mall   her nose pressed against the window
Looking into the consuming world   "Buy whatever you
want"   as if dreams come true   what's the price   enter her
room at night and carry her into his bed   more offers   a
home   a car   a marriage   a green card   he snoring   bad
breath   stare into space   sleep less   indigestion of the soul
no sense of direction   sit staring at her hands   infected with

130

athlete's foot   suddenly see them wet   teardrops   what?
no!   no time for pity   too proud to sell   move to Harlem
where she belongs   different root   same fate. $100
through a Chinese girlfriend   married for green card
thought she could settle down for a while   but in the third
week someone turned the key in the lock at midnight   the
owner   no   the lover of the Chinese girl   back from an
interview in San Francisco   sold for a hundred   no more
girlfriend   not available   another offer   one night shelter
and a screw   "stinky meat" she was told after the business
in the dark   long after   tongue in the cheek   no speech
possible   suddenly she realizes   gradually I realize   so
much need for love   no time for love   this awful thought
drifting in and out   make it stop   God is love   What?   no!
no God for Chinese   sick of belief   but this need for love
no money for love   that December afternoon   roaming
along Fifth Avenue   a job   waitress   bus girl   cashier   a
place to stay   a bowl of instant noodles   grabbing at the
straw   nothing there   on to the next   in the December
snow   no sense of direction   feelings dismissed   how she
survived   but this roar   this voice in her skull   this need to
be loved   falling on her face   in the first snow   tender
mercies   in the December snow   in the unheated base-
ment   Jackson Heights   first night   flooded bathroom
floating mattress   yeast infection   punishment for the sin
face in her hands   avoiding a curious rat   on the eve of the
Chinese New   what?   no?   OK   on the eve of Christ
no?   what?   New Year?   Good God!   sorry   good heaven
no God for Chinese   New Year's Eve   a rat sitting on my
face   waiting   silence   Big Apple rising   trumpets blow-
ing   something wet in hands   hers probably   no one else
around   except for the rat   dear rat   Happy New Year
phone ringing   her sponsor's call   "ungrateful beast"
telling the story of the Harlem apartment to a journalist

how can Chinese betray Chinese   shame   no more connec-
tion   she is on her own   she has been on her own   only
pretending she has someone behind her   Big Apple rising
no more dreams   no head   no brain   no sense of direction
only the sequence of the apartments   six   what?   ten
Good God   sorry   good heavens   memories fading   last
stop Flushing address   life recycles   time compressed
fragments of names   being achieves silence   images inca-
pable of repose   asserting like mad   recognizable even
burned into ashes   clinging to the threshold   one has to
believe something   face in her hands   tender mercies
on New Year's Eve   no sense of direction   no direction.

西藏

那个人在我眼里他时候都已经不存在了。对这
山。
那从边到那，果同有一些展长的头发。
　　　　抖着卷儿。算是一种绐中看，
一束儿，叫着这儿越来越扁。再不扁，
有些习惯化了。
膝盖搂吗不痒。
我守有咱边相互之间不描述我们；
　　　和你有限两手空空地来描述。
二十五年之间只有一次指着上面的到时是长我
粗。
哪一轨地隔段舞步中么你之么明那。

Wei Se is three-quarters Tibetan and one-quarter Chinese. She was born in Lhasa in 1966, and graduated from the Southwestern National Institute in Sechuan in 1988. She is the editor of the magazine Tibetan Literature, and a member of the Tibetan branch of the Chinese Writers Association.

请注意他们的眼睛日多黑少，一闪眼即灭。

精神在物质之上。

在剩休路上，菊花、珠狼依次出现。

原地踏步一下，原地就不是原地了。

山是山。水是水。酥油、糌粑是他们的主食了。

看见那么个奇妙的地方，

就想搭起帐篷，

哪晚唱得嗓子断了，

叫我怎能不想你！

雪化得很慢。他又何必别我而去。

宝贝在自己家里都不觉得稀奇，如今，到处也就逐渐普及。

一支香一直燃到今天。

喂请猜看，找不到他的人怎么办？怎么办？

唱要唱个够。跳要跳个够。

　西藏文学

From *The String of Beads, Fate*

VI

Now it should be spring.
The new leaves look clean.
You should be a young woman, just blossoming,
but on the thin surface of a foreign land
you have grown old too fast,
running, untimely, back and forth
between pride and sorrow.
Tears cling to your cheeks.
A string of beads
under the tree bending with too much fruit.
Whose body scrapes the flagstone?
Whose hands are twisting the beads?

They belong to your previous life,
alone and free,
a kasaya over the boiling dust.
It's the same string of beads.
Why do you refuse to pick them up?
What are you clutching in your hands?

From outside the monastery, sounds of your previous life
are trying to enter your ears.

VII

Kneeling
between two monasteries,
a six-word mantra,
forehead touching the dusty earth.
The force of the beads.

The living Buddha, fifteen years old,
speaks a foreign language.
Outside the temple, a tree.
Inside, a tower encrusted with jewels.
Forty thousand Buddhas,
forty thousand Tibetan words,
forty thousand leaves,
all fall on your shoulders.

Between the two monasteries
your clothing disappears.
When will your silence, endless, ever reach the shore?
The circle of your present life,
encircled by a string of beads, predestined,
breaks the surface of the darkness.

Tibet

When I saw him he was already gone. Right here.
From here to there, strands of long hair
flutter against the wind. Streamers of sutra.
A beam of light flares, then dies.

Some snow is melting.
Knees hurt?
I'd rather fall out between hadas.
Or tell stories with empty hands.
See how darkness fills their eyes, melts in the mouth.
Spirit above matter.
Lotus and nectar on the pilgrim road.
One step and you're no longer where you were.
Mountain, water. Yak butter and zanba for my food.
I want to raise my tent
in a perfect place,
but the rope is broken.

The snow is melting slowly, but there's no need
to race against the day.
No one values the treasure,
which once stolen is too late to regret.
The incense is still burning.
What should those who lost their gods do? Guess!
Sing and dance to your heart's satisfaction.
We die of small wounds and are resurrected.
A spider is spinning its web to the sound of sutra.
Simple landscape in the thin air.

A horse takes you to the destination.
Horses have run away from the grasslands,
half of them already gone.
Not theirs but the riders' hearts are empty.
People circle and circle.

When I turn my head suddenly, he is not there.
Where is the road?
I get rich from selling beads.
I brought someone into his garden
and found a brass spoon in the village.
A blessing disguised or a curse disguised?
I drift along with my days,
the sun too big, too black.
In my sleep, people arrive.
Some will follow others till death;
they leave with the rich. Buckets of tears pour down.
When you disappear,
don't forget to take your shoes and your hat.

Words that float in the air cast blue shadows.
You look great in Tibetan clothes, like a banner.
The high land barley is no good for brewing beer anymore,
but we all smack our lips to praise its taste.
Om Mani Padme Hum.
If the place is fun, we'll settle down
and drink any tea that tastes sweet.

Damn! Why are you pregnant again?
The leaves are falling. So what's up?
Grab an instrument and let her try it.
His deformed face is smeared with tears.
"Wake up, wake up," says the baby.
I know him.

The day he was born, a huge mushroom popped up
outside the door.
On his left palm, the image of an eye.
Thinking she could no longer stay in this world,
his mother left.

Snow, why are you melting so slowly?
Waiting for good weather, they finally lost patience.
Only I remain, like this,
neither here nor there.
The swamp west of Lhasa used to be a killing ground,
ghastly at night.
I'm in love with the only language I know.
But where are my beads?

The man with the deformed head is still weeping,
but no one minds.
In this world, we can't retrieve even a single hair.
So we dream.

书籍

西川

应当用火把照亮书籍，像印加人
用火把照亮他们的城市

石砌的城市，火把照亮它的
织物、长矛和金银器皿

些许时间用以考证自身的东西
从敌对到团结，把纯正的秘密揭开

像赫拉克利特与柏拉图
被书页的同一只蜜蜂吸引

"所有的书是同一本书"
女性化的雪莱几乎这样说道

所有的错误是同样的错误
像托勒密探索大地与星辰

追逐精确的计算
得出荒谬的结论

书籍构成了比书籍更大的空间
大火熊熊将断送它自己

亲切呈出没于图书馆的味道
如阿尔博斯·赫胥黎

一个被大火剥夺了信笺的人
在情感的颠沛中提炼了余生

Xi Chuan was born in Xuzhou, Jiangsu, in 1963, and graduated from Beijing University in 1985. He is now the editor of the Xinhua News Agency's *Globe Magazine* in Beijing. His work has appeared in the magazines *Chinese Writers*, *Guangxi Literature*, *October*, *People's Literature*, *Poetry*, and *World Literature*. His poem "Rainy Season" won October's 1987 Literary Award.

没看到沉睡的玫瑰
在坐落满（死亡巫跳送样）

巍峨的书架被压弯
不堪那沉睡的千万个灵魂

我与千万个灵魂同居一室
像巫隐在心灵的火花了

寂静，否定的因素，说吧——
我打开一本书，一个灵魂就苏醒

一座我从未进入的城市
立着我从未见过的女人

一个我从未进入的黄昏
有斗牛生的芳香忽奄奄一息

罗密欧的愤怒、哈姆雷特的良心
随意说出的真理、抑郁的神吟

我阅读一个家族的预言
我看到的幸福并不比痛苦更多

历史仅记录少数人的丰功伟绩
其他人说话汇合为沉默

1991.6.

For Haizi*

You didn't have time to create the perfect spring,
yet you hurried to lay a foundation for song
so sacred it destroys the singer.
In your singing we see the sun rising, the heavens falling,
wheat ripening in the southern wind,
an eagle flying across the fields, night in its mouth.

Tears. Evening light. Distant songs.
It's getting dark, and my sisters have returned
to their rooms.
Constellations point to the west; someone mute
searches for a friend,
watches new wood added to an old fire.
In the ashes life continues:
Today's gain less than tonight's loss.

The voice of my pain grows quiet,
then joins the deeper silence that night requires.
Every nature has its gloom.
In 1989 you touched
the dewy face of death,
and departed—not dead but sacrificed.
Your silence is not silence but song.

To change is all flesh can do,
the body still ignorant but the soul no longer full of hate.
The person who sleeps in the fields
will become the first grain of wheat in the barn.
The day-traveler
will hear gods talking in the sky.
The soul, following peach blossoms and torches,
has a chance to fly
into the light.

In a drizzling autumn dawn,
I dreamed about you again, as a youth,
your empty hands stroking the dirty stone of the archangel,
your singing lips kissing the barren soil of your homeland.
You should have gone back to your hut,
scented with Indian incense,
to love and marry,
to write at your leisure about despair.

In the distance the empty sea shivers.
The sky is deep, heaven invisible.
It was a lonely soul that died in the wheat fields,
soaked in evening light.
Who whispered in your ear
"It's time"? Who appeared before you
and opened the path that leads into the night?
Ah, it's time,
it's past time—now dawn salutes you.

*Haizi was a young Chinese poet who committed
suicide in 1989.

Books

Books should be illuminated by torches,
just as the Incas illuminated their city.

Torches shone on its
woven fabric, pears, gold and silver utensils—

objects that time uses to express itself
from opposition to unity, revealing the secret of fate,

like Hercules and Plato
attracted by the same spring bee.

"All books are the same book,"
pale Mallarmé said with confidence.

All mistakes are the same mistake,
like Ptolemy's research into earth and stars,

his precise calculations
that only led him to absurd conclusions.

Books create a space larger than books.
The life of fire ends in its own flame.

Emperor Qin Shi haunted the library hallway
and Aldous Huxley,

robbed of the past by a fire,
clarified the rest of his life in a single lecture.

I see a rose
covered with dust; what else can death do?

XI CHUAN

The lofty bookshelves sag
under thousands of sleeping souls.

We live together,
hiding beneath the spirit's torch.

Silence, hopeful—
every time I open a book, a soul is awakened.

A strange woman walks
in a city I've never seen.

A funeral is taking place
in a dusk I've never entered.

Othello's anger, Hamlet's conscience,
Truth spoken at will, muffled bells.

I read a family prophecy.
The pains I've seen are no more than the pains themselves.

History records only a few people's deeds:
The rest is silence.

Birds

Birds are the sky's language.
Their songs suggest silence.
Black birds may appear suddenly,
which doesn't prevent
a wounded bird
from approaching eternity.

Birds come out in the sun.
Birds come out in the moonlight.
Flying soil,
crystal of memory.
Flames can't go higher than wings,
Sky can't come lower.

In the longing of the birds
trees rise from the earth.
In the longing of the birds
fruits tower in the clouds.
A city made of rocks
allows them holidays of love.

I have seen such birds
fly out of sight with seeds in their mouths.
But every morning
there's always one bird
circling above my head,
an angel in holiday dress.

That's the bird in my dream
whose job it is to watch over the earth.
Stars pour in through its body.
A lone man's world
almost equals the world of the gods.
Our ecstasy is our loss.

Bats in the Twilight

In Goya's painting, flying up and down
left to right, they bring nightmares
to artists, but their whispers
never wake them.

An ineffable happiness appears
on their human faces: faux birds
whose black bodies
blend into the darkness
but whose seeds will never sprout.

Without hope of salvation,
blind, cruel,
they hang upside down on trees
like withered leaves,
led by their will.

They may force a sleepwalker to join them,
grab the torch from his hand, put it out.
They may also throw an invading wolf
into a valley, speechless.

At night, if a child refuses to sleep,
it must be that a bat
has sneaked out of a night-watcher's eye
to tell him about fate.

Can penniless bats bring
us prosperity? The moon's waxing and waning
plucks out their hair, ugly and anonymous.

Their iron hearts touch me.
On a summer evening
I pass by my old neighborhood and see kids playing,
a large flock of bats flying around their heads.

The sun going down spreads its shadow across the lane.
Over the street
golden bats
hover in silence.

The bats
are memory
urging me to linger
here in the lane where I grew up,
here in the lane where I was a child.

怀旧

雪迪

站在凸地上往回看的人
看见青春是钉在土里的铁钉
祖国是一片带不走的土地
双亲衰老，远离；在那里
是一堵倒塌的墙
家是一块吊在勾子上的肉
童年这把弯刀向上，童年
木头的把在回忆里腐朽
站在凸地上向前看
洼地均匀地排列
象畜群在异乡人回头的时刻
集体做爱。象孤单的
怀旧者，听见身子底下
上来的一次一次叫喊

1994

Xue Di was born in Beijing in 1957. His published works include *Heart Into Soil* (Burning Deck Press & Lost Roads Publishers, 1998), *Flames* (Paradigm Press, 1995), *Trembling* (Workers Publishing House, Beijing, 1989) and Dream Talk (Lijiang Publishing, Guangxi, 1988). Xue Di is a two-time recipient of the Hellman/Hammett Award, sponsored by the Fund for Free Expression, an affiliate of Human Rights Watch, New York. Since shortly after the Tienanmen Square Massacre in 1989, he has been a fellow in Brown University's Freedom to Write Program in Providence, Rhode Island.

Interplay

The living
are shadows of the dead
They make noise
When the dead dream in the silent dark
when the dead wake
the living feel sudden terror
day-long loneliness
It is the dead
who have left home
to meet their family on the way
The living, day by day, age
It is the dead who try to
return to the world
The living feel alone
when they meet each other
They shout "Who
loves me?"
It is the dead standing
next to them
The dead clench their teeth
with contempt
with revenge
because the living
are always giving the dead a bad name

XUE DI

The Passage to Heaven

I see him from a distance. Sleep
is a long narrow train with
many empty seats. I see myself
sitting, traveling somewhere
Along the way, on my left
I see unfold, meticulously, a
mysterious orange and ochre scape. I
almost wake up
Heaven is just back of my
eyes, almost as if—the train moving
just a bit faster or
stopping—I might become
the first person to see heaven
and return. I can't tell you
how that passage woke me at midnight and made
me happy. The train reaches its
destination in the tropics. I'm
waking slowly and longing for
two women I love

Nostalgia

A man looks back on the land as it
rises. He sees youth as
nails hammered into the dust. Motherland
is the land he can't take with him
Parents distant, decrepit. Wall
collapsing. Home is a
hunk of meat on a hook
Childhood a butcher knife raised, wooden handle
decaying memory. A man
looks forward to the land as it rises
the hollows running primly
As the stranger turns his head, herds
of animals are mating. The man
lonely, nostalgic
hears screams, and again
rising from below, screams

诗句系列　　　　严力

我的同胞终于在他们哭过很久的地方
开始造盐

我递出一张鸟的名片
请把电话打给远走高飞

生命最终是一块雕死的木头
曾经被绿叶生长过

爱情迟早会在我磕掉了门牙的地方
镶上一块糖

我的视线在她胸前被绞成了两团毛线

人类是人类的遗迹

Born in Beijing, 1954,
Yan Li started writing
poetry in 1973 and
painting in 1979.
He soon became a
member of the Stars,
an avant-garde
Beijing art group.
He founded (in 1987)
the poetry magazine
First Line in New
York City. His major
poetry collections
include *This Poem
Is Probably Not Bad,*
(Shulin Press, Taiwan,
1991); *Selected
Poems,* (First Line
Press, New York,
1990); and *Selected
Poems* 1976-1985
(Yongyu Printing,
Taiwan, 1990). A
collection of prose
works, *I've Become
a Scum Who Loves
Himself Most,* was
published by Nine
Song Press (Taiwan,
1990).

From *Serial Poetic*

We have the power to change ourselves.
We can't behave worse than people.
Today we are nothing but tools for science.
To walk past the grave, we must make some noise.
She is gone,
together with the sky above my head.
The plane crashed
because it ran out of sky.

A mood so sharp
no sheath can hold it.

The psychology of wearing underwear outside the jacket
is proof that national self-respect surpasses
human self-respect

The world walks by, dressed in luxury.
In my eyes there's nothing but two rolls of
blank film.
Poetry peeks into the body
to see what the nude is wearing on the inside.

The artist often leans out, stretched
between two extremes,
shouting for help with exquisite slogans.

A failed love affair is full of troubled vitamins.

If you are in a place that has two suns
the first thing you must do is to select a shadow.

Flowers don't know how to make room for the gardener.

With great care and shining eyes
he puts the fishbone back into the tank,
believing that he hasn't harmed the soul of the fish.

The flesh of darkness approaches the night
between my teeth.
I see how its bestiality chews your mouth into pieces
but that has nothing to do with your kiss.

On holidays
you hold me in your hand like a balloon,
the hope of your breath bursting through me.

Conscience is a murderer,
burying my violent thoughts before they come out.
My body is a cemetery, overcrowded.
Occasionally I think of visiting,
but that thought flashes once then subsides.

In my body's drawer
mice play with my guns, which go off accidentally,
hitting the roaches who are reading my secret documents.

Winter besieges the remaining protein.
We show as much interest in nutrition as in spring.

The broken bridge in the painting proves
that all history is crossed by swimming.

Today is not a good day for sex
because
tomorrow in a northern bed I'll sleep with spring.

You say too many days have been drowned by sunlight.
You suggest living like underground water,
but I know
that every second, people turn on the tap.

After being wounded many times
he realizes he hasn't become a hero,
so he fantasizes about the future:
how to squeeze into a museum
with those calluses on his toes.

My dear,
don't let other people butter your bread.

Fruit knife,
why don't you take a rest?
Adam has bitten the apple.
My feet have wiped up the rain with sunshine.
A triumphant destination awaits me on the road,
but I don't want to eat the best food too early,
so I've been lingering along the road for years,
maybe even longer.

Curses line both of the sidewalks
like the trees which make our city green.

I love freedom
but the cage is always too big for me.

If a poet could call for poems to be delivered
when he is hungry, then all the take-out restaurants
would be bookstores.

YAN LI

Imagine men and women every night
crossing the border between clothes and flesh.
what kind of territorial problems
could not be solved on earth?

You jump out of your pants
into the tomb.
your plan to rape death is not even forty years old.
I'd think you could wait another few years.
Between you and me,
except for the unspoken
it's pointless to say anything.

The baby's kisses rest like two kiwis on the mother's chest.

Since childhood I have believed that fire lives in wood
and that the door won't open unless you knock.

The American dream forces me to sleep even during the day.

Perhaps when the aliens see pictures of human beings
they'll think they are treasures right off the printing press.

Only young people know their faces are the
    address books of youth.
They squeeze out pimples to make room for new entries.

So much happiness,
but a sudden movement could destroy it forever.

On New Year's Eve
human beings flatten the earth another inch.

With its gun of flowers
spring holds the butterflies hostage
in its own garden.

The needle of love
sews up all my senses.

The door keeps the ego in its mouth
like a piece of candy
unaware of its own sweetness.

If earth were no longer a virgin
I wouldn't care to get pregnant.

I love to listen to the frogs
loudly reading the layers of duckweed.
Love is a most loyal whirlpool
that has never abandoned my boat.

Chicken or egg?
I've been arguing this problem with God till midnight,
which is when one of us suddenly falls asleep.

Ever since freedom got the fax number for my soul,
a piece of white paper has been arriving every day.

You are like the light bulb
screwed into the socket of a disconnected lamp
and I am its delicate shade.

车过黄河

伊 沙

列车正经过黄河
我正在厕所小便
我深知这不该
我 应该坐在窗前
或站在车门旁边
左手叉腰
右手作眉檐
眺望 像个伟人
至少像个诗人
想点河上的事情
或历史的陈账
那时人们都在眺望
我在厕所里
时间很长
现在这时间属于我
我等了一天一夜
只一泡尿功夫
黄河已经流远

Yi Sha, who is of both Han and Kazak nationality, was born in Sichuan in 1966. Since graduating from the Chinese Department of Beijing Teachers' College, he has been teaching at the Xian Foreign Language Institute. His poems have appeared in magazines in China, Hong Kong, Malaysia, the Philippines, Singapore, and Taiwan. His book of poems *Starve the Poets* was published by the Huaqiao Press in Beijing in 1994. Some of his work has been translated into English and German, among other languages. He is the editor of the poetry magazine *Feifei*.

The Train Crossed the Yellow River

When the train crossed the Yellow River
I was pissing in the bathroom.
I knew I shouldn't—
I should be sitting at the window
or standing at the door,
left hand on hip,
right hand shading my brow,
looking far into the distance
like a great man—
at least like a poet—
pondering the river
or some moment in history.
Everyone else was doing it.
I alone stayed in the bathroom
for ages.
Right now time belonged to me.
I had waited a day and a night:
A stream of piss
and the Yellow River flowed on

Neighbors

A lesbian couple
lives next door,
protected
by the free air of our country.
They're more honest
and happier
than I, a bachelor scrounging every day for food.
Their wanton laughter from morning till night
makes my life miserable.
In an age when the wolves outnumber the sheep,
what a waste
to let these two girls alone.
I often think about how to rescue them,
but every time I knock on their door
pretending I need to borrow some soy sauce,
they answer in unison: "Meiyou!" "No way!"
One day I listened outside their window.
What I heard really depressed me; they
were talking about men.
The word "dirty" came up,
as did "garbage."

That Year

That year in Shanghai,
I often lost my way
along the river,
saw many
strange banners,
a man's hand
and a woman's,
clasped.
I heard the sound of bells for the first time,
unsettling
but also soothing.
That year
I stared at the sunset
among the city's mountains.
I learned how to flee
when something happened.
That year
I saw myself
as in a foreign movie,
crying miserably.
Since then I've held my head high
among the crowds.
That year an electrician
asked me for directions
to the new buildings.
My neighbor Aunt Shen
cursed me non-stop
because I had by accident stepped
on her daughter's shadow.
That year I heard
birds singing.
That year was 1977.

Yi Sha

I stood on the Waibaidu Bridge,
watching boats in the Suzhou River,
searching for the little sampan
that had brought me here.

The North Wind Was Blowing

The north wind was blowing.
In the open air I was watching a movie,
the story of "The White-haired Girl,"
the revolutionary ballet,
and my jaw dropped.
Was I really that educated?
Was my soul purified?
Snowflakes were drifting.
Which is more beautiful,
revolution or ballet?
The landlord has now raped Xi'er,
and she has taken the red-tasseled spear in her hands.
Somehow in a dark corner
my little cock
stood at attention for the first time—
proof that I'd grown up
and was ready to carry on the Revolution.

YI SHA

I Write What History Cannot Write

June 1989, and the university campus
was like a deserted city
after an air-raid drill.
Tired of playing, the children had evacuated the place—
classrooms empty, offices empty,
freedom for student lovers.
My girlfriend and I retreated
behind curtains in the women's dormitory
to make love: At this moment in history
this docile girl had suddenly become brave.
I pressed forward without hesitation.
The white sheet stained with her blood
was a banner—the last one at the funeral
outside the window, fluttering against the wind.
The sharp ache of history passed through me
and into my girlfriend's heart.
Those days we hovered between life and death.
The sun still rose as usual.
Those days in the wake of June 1989
we lived life to the full,
itching for change.

This Fall This Year

I can't stop the autumn.
I can't stop the leaves from fluttering to the earth.
I can't stop
the sheet of newspaper
from drifting through the wind
like a banner of mourning.
An old man sits on a park bench
with a cane.
I can't keep him
from thinking of the Soviet Union
with bitter nostalgia.

赞美劳动

于坚

我赞美劳动
我赞美一个劳动者
他手臂上的肌肉鼓出来　抡动着锤子
他把黑炭砸碎　引下腰去
几粒火种　膛亮他粗糙的手
爆裂成一炉真正的火火焰
火光照亮了他的脸
把铁石和整个作坊照亮
劳动　就这样开始
他干的活　是浇铸　打以铁链
他在车间不看这些链子
他也不想　它们将会有什么用途
这是劳动　一气呵成和流传的过程
浇铸的是手和工具
把一把铜坯投进火炉
浇铸我另外一把
高举的拳头　锤子
从炽红的火星中出来　成为折的铁链
他的表情和动作没有任何与心情有关的暗示
他只是一组被劳动牵引的肌肉
只是随着工具的运动而产生的线条
唯一的含意　就是劳动

1989. 12月

Yu Jian was born
in 1954 in Kunming.
When he was two,
an overdose of
streptomycin for his
pneumonia caused
permanent hearing
damage. He
graduated from
the Chinese
Department of
Yunnan University,
and in 1984 founded
They, an under-
ground poetry maga-
zine, to which many
New Generation
poets contributed.
His first collection, 60
Poems, was published
in 1989 by Yunnan
People's Publishing.

In Praise of Work

I praise work
I praise the worker
The muscles bulge in his arms
He swings a hammer to break coal
He bends.
A few sparks escape his rough hands
and shoot into the furnace
The fire brightens his face
his anvil and his workshop
To cast steel chains
this is how
the work begins

He doesn't need them
He doesn't think of their future
Just work a process of smelting and casting
Hands and tools take over
throwing steel bars into the furnace
to become something else
The abandoned plowshares and hammers
emerge from the burning coal as new chains
He is a surgeon
extracting chains from scrap iron
turning it into something useful
His movements and expressions suggest nothing
He is a system of
muscles controlled by the work
The motion of the tools moves his body
the only meaning work

The Fence

The red land   thirty-five acres or so   at the bottom
    of the hill

On the slope grow pine trees   grass and mushrooms

A wooden cottage   an ox head hangs from the window ledge
In the front yard firewood   footprints   dogs and a
    muddy plow
The host not in sight   the plowed red soil looks fertile

The sound of a stream seems to come from
    behind the mountain
This is a place for the gods everything splendid
except for a piece of fence in the middle of a field
    instead of around the house—
crooked   about ten branches tied together with vines
standing over there   fencing in nothing   surrounded
    by nothing
If it went a few steps back   it might create
    a vegetable garden
Or if it extended further between the meadow
    and the new soil
it could become a sign of possession
But it stands where it's not supposed to be
firmly planted in the middle of the red field far away from
    the edge of everything
It isn't a statue in a square   but a piece of fence
The cottage has often appeared in my dreams
but I never expected this extra piece of fence
which makes me feel unsatisfied   anxious to correct it
It has nothing to do with me though—
I'm just passing through
This place is for the gods and for them
in the middle of this red land
that piece of fence belongs

178

I Overheard Them Talking about the Source of the Pearl River

On a fifth floor in the city of Qujing
they were talking about the Pearl River and its source
"We were there two years ago   fifty miles away from the city
Nothing to see there
not a tree   not a soul   no grass   no road
only some rocks
big and small   all gray   The mud sucked at our shoes
Some crows flew up out of nowhere   almost scared
        us to death
What bad luck!
After a long trek in the mud   we reached a ditch
A drop of water
dripped down from a crack in the rocks   This is the source
        of the Pearl River
What bad luck!   We'll never go again in this life "
In the City of Qujing   I listened to them talking
        about the Pearl River
and looked into the distance   there were only barren hills

YU JIAN

Power Outage

In our life power outages are common
A little dumb show of the fuse   the power plant's arthritis
    the legalized rape and violence
and the bright gallows   We take all of these
    for granted   calmly
When the lights blink out   and the world goes dark
we don't panic   doing what we have to do as usual
Everyone knows a power outage won't change the size
    of a room
or change the amount of starch in bread   or the
    color of water
We know everything remains the same   before and after—
the process   the details   the part   the whole   the climax
    and the end   nothing changes
First some romantic tricks ghosts   a corpse
    a haunted house
the candles in the dark kingdom   the footsteps on the
    stairways and the monsters
These little images attack us   We pretend to be scared
    throwing our hands up or throwing our chests out
We know these tricks as well as our toys   our milk and MSG
We know that our doors are safely locked   our neighbors are
    comrades   and the gate is guarded
Finally we all stay where we are   safe and sound   in the
    same position   with the same thoughts
still the same good people   still maintaining the same good
    manners and self-restraint
No one will ever suddenly attack a woman
"like a sword" (this happens only in fiction)   During the
    power outage the world is as perfect as before
The watcher is still watching   the doer still doing the
    meditator still meditating

180

Our hands and feet can still stretch freely　no need to stand
　　on tiptoe like invaders
Everything is the same　space　color　voice　texture
　　weight and heart
the chandelier above　the floor below　the left hand on the
　　left　the right hand on the right
the bed in the corner　near the window　next to the
　　dresser and mirror
the trunk on top　the shoes at the bottom　the food
　　in the cabinet
The left hand can reach aspirin and thermos
　　glass and cigarettes
The right hand can get oranges　box of candy　magazines
　　a bit farther there are matches
Half a step forward　I can touch the sofa　it sinks as I sit
Behind me　six feet up on the blank wall　hang pictures
My parents and me　the smile of 1954 still there the 1967
　　chair still there
A bookshelf next to the door　classics on the top　medical
　　books on the third shelf
The wallpaper dates from the year of the Horse　the bricks
　　in the wall from 1947
The ice is in the refrigerator　the clothes in the closet　the
　　water in the pipe　the time behind the clock's glass
Soft is the cloth　sharp is the fruit knife　loud is the noise
　　itchy is my skin
The sheets are white　the ink is black　the rope is long
　　the blood is liquid
My shoes cost a yuan　the electricity five cents a
　　kilowatt-hour my watch eighty yuan　the television
　　five hundred
Everything is still here　nothing disappears　The electricity
　　is gone　but the switch remains

181

the meter remains   the tools remain   the electrician   the
    engineer and the map remain
The only thing that's gone is the wolf   the wolf as featured
    on the August calendar
It disappears into the darkness at the moment of
    the power outage
I can't see it
I don't know if it's still on the paper   for a few seconds
I feel it breathing and listening in the flat darkness
This feeling is the only illusion   the only distraction from my
    calmness and alertness when the power goes out—
the only illusion   in the midsummer night I shudder

Thank You Father

Twelve months a year
poppy flowers bloom in your pipe
A warm family   they never divorce
never look for trouble   never borrow money   never
    laugh aloud
quiet as mice   cleaner than a hospital
The ancestors' virtue   smooth as pebbles
never bleeds   In the flooding century
its designs become more simple
As a father you brought home bread and salt
At the long black table you sat in the middle
The seat that belongs to emperors professors and leaders
Your sons sat at your sides   they were not negotiators
but your golden buttons made you shine
From your seat you stroked us   your eyes full of love
like a stomach   warm and persistent
teaching me how to be a man
You used to have stomach aches
When you were in pain   your sons became beetles
    helpless   insignificant

We were together from morning to night   but I never
    saw your back
I didn't see your resumé till I grew up
"active and hard working   warm and honest   amiable and
    easy to approach
respects authority   never complains   never leaves early"
Once you told me you liked football when you were young
as well as dancing   especially the two-step
I was startled   as if you were talking about a sea lion

I knew as a child that you were a good person   These days
there are more bad guys than good guys on the streets
When those heathens were arrested   exiled
      and gone forever
you walked out of the park and became a bridegroom

In 1957   you became a father
As a good person   Father   how hard your life was
confess   denounce   inform
after you'd done all these   you went home with
      your suitcase
At night you couldn't sleep   always listening carefully
or getting up   to examine our diaries and dreams
as seriously as the Gestapo
Your own children were like tigers   they worried you
Any impertinent remarks might implicate relatives
You stood in line till midnight to buy coal and exchange the
      rationed cooking oil for milk
You traveled to Shanghai   enduring the hardship
      to buy us clothing
You made friends with doctors   drivers   and guards
Experienced and astute   always flexible   smooth
in the dark age   a time of turmoil   you brought me
      up like this
and got me an identity card
Finally I grew up   not an easy job   Father   I've become a
      man   exactly like you
hard-working   simply dressed   immaculate

As a baby I looked like a hard luck case
I might have lost my sanity and died of encephalitis
or been crushed under a truck while crossing against
    a red light
or been misled by hoodlums and sent to prison
or been addicted to drinking   drugs   gambling
    or got AIDS
But Father   I'm involved in none of these
    not even masturbation
I don't travel far away from my parents
I study hard and progress every day
go to bed at nine-thirty   do my laundry on Sunday
I remained a virgin till 28 and passed the physical
    before my wedding
Three-bedroom apartment   living with parents
    children all fine
The family sits around the dining room table
    as warm as spring
This is not an easy job   my captain
my white-haired father   not an easy job

Mouse

That self-invited little bastard has moved into my room
coming and going like a shadow   never face to face with me
I didn't know you were a star
until I saw you on TV   with Donald Duck
No more peace
A gray mouth has come into my room
like a tumor growing in my body
After many X-rays the doctors can't find anything
My bread is half-nibbled
my rice has suspicious black spots
Who is the culprit?
Carefully I listen—
outside the closet   on the floor
I hear the small harsh sound
But I'm not sure
if you   you little bastard   are chewing my favorite shirt
or my grandfather's antiques
You rustle around
as if showing your concern
like my grandmother
who used to get up at midnight to close the window for me
You dance on my cake   pee on my pills
and gnaw my books into scraps
But after all you don't know which object will make noise
when you knock down a vase or jump across something
causing a small earthquake
that startles me from a nightmare   Standing on tiptoe
I can't even get mad
Gently I feel my way from bed to bookshelf
afraid you'll hear me
as if you were writing   and couldn't be disturbed
Clumsier than you I knock a chair over

Anxious   guilty   I look around
Maybe you have fallen asleep you bastard
or drunk some milk   changed the room
In the darkness you roll your black beady eyes
watching me   big and stupid   naked   ill-mannered

You keep quiet
about my appearance at night   unlike my father
Such virtue makes me feel embarrassed
In the end I can no longer stand it   so I knock and poke
        blindly
making a thorough search   to catch you   and sentence you
But seeing the gigantic furniture
the innumerable mouse shelters
I'm terribly upset and at a loss
The only thing to do is give up
My friends all think that since I live alone
I must be calm and focused in my studies
Actually I'm always too worried to go out
As soon as I hurry home after work
I open my closet and suitcases
to see what this clever little bastard
has done now

YU JIAN

From *The Brown Notebook: Rejecting Metaphor*

We have forgotten language Metaphor becomes a means of
    transportation disguising itself as poetry
Language games become life games Metaphor equals mask
Chinese culture is a "metaphor culture"
Poetry today rejects metaphor
This restores poetry's naming power
Real poetry rejects readers It rejects the reading habit
    not reading itself
Poetry is not a noun but a verb
Poetry is its own reason for being Poetry begins from
    language and ends in language
Rejection and depth: Reject "instinct" "inspiration"
    or "passion"
Poetry doesn't express emotions It is a process of the mind
Don't wait for inspiration Control language
Genuine writing is the most subjective and the most rational
The process of writing poetry is the process of
    cleaning out garbage
A poet is not a genius or a romantic prince or a martyr
A poet is a worker in a factory a language operator
To write real poetry is to refuse every metaphor
Poetry provides a language fact eliminate imagination
    eliminate romanticism eliminate metaphor
Poetry is not a way of observing life It is a way of living life
Poetry mocks those who look for "depth" and "essence"
Poetry is naming It's as simple as that
Return to where the language came from Return to the time
    before metaphor
How? I can't answer It's poetry

188

结束，

完成之后又怎样？在那白昼
我把幼儿举到空中，又回到
最初的中心点，象一株树
迅从地下涌来使我升高
现在我睁开崭新的眼睛
并对天长叹：完成之后又怎样？

看呵，不要轻过你们的脸
七天成为一个星期跟随我
无数次成功的梦在我的周
贮满着敦的梦，于是一个不被理解的
苦难奇异瑞倪，并被重新
写进天空：完成之后又怎样？

永无休止，其面音象一条先见的路
所有的力努射入致命的脚踵，在那里
我不再知道：完成之后又怎样？
但空气中有另一声吉的白无误
理所当然这仅是最后的问题
却无人回答：完成之后又怎样？

我不再关心，我的隐秘之贴心
更加透明象相的荟辖
永远期待结束但你们隐忍不语
一架飞犀使我倾心信托里定的方向
整个冬天我都在小声地问：希冀例地
微笑，谁终告诉我：
完成之后又怎样？

1984.

Zhai Yongming was
born in Chendu,
Sichuan, in 1955.
From 1974 to 1976,
she worked in the
countryside, and in
1980 she graduated
from the Chendu
Electric
Communication
Engineering Institute.
Her collection of
poems is called
Woman (Lijiang
Publishing, 1988).
She lives in Chendu.

Café Song

I. Afternoon

Sad and lingering
on Fifth Avenue
in a café
with a little door
under a street corner lamp.

To sit by the window
and sip the bald owner's black coffee
and think "How many people have passed by unnoticed
going to work, going home."

Bored, we talk about love:
"Yesterday I wish
it was yesterday."
A nostalgic song drifting back and forth.

No time to clear
the throat clogged with coffee and truth.
Our tongues in and out
rolling around obscure words.

The men's names get bigger
like an officer's order to charge.
The stiff formula on the blackboard
frightens me.

You whisper in my ear
about great adventures and mysteries.
"Laughing is better than weeping...
Let's keep going...."

Then the silence.
A couple sits down.
They're from another state living
a lethargic pastoral life.

Someone says "This playboy could have been
a great hero—Now
his hair is thinning."
I bend my head to drink my coffee.

People get drunk and exchange partners
to kill another afternoon
while I keep wondering
what's the problem?
With your perfect accent
You're still talking about your children, your great job,
your heavenly community.

Dusk arrives   alluring candles.
On the radio
someone sings
"Strangers...strangers."

II. Evening

Disco blasts
through the flicker of candles
from the speakers
like two cheekbones
at the sides of the room.

White and black evening dresses.
A bewitching woman at the next table.
From the corner of her eye she catches
his loving gaze.

No one notices a third table
where three men and two women
discuss their identity crisis
like ghosts—
It reminds me of
a Chinese restaurant at the North Pole.
One of them interrupts: "My wife is studying
international finance."

Different races.
Serious talk
foaming with pathetic color
like stale beer.

Someone's thinking
"Where can I find
a permanent bed?"
His serious face is lost in the darkness.

ZHAI YONGMING

I'm measuring
the happiness
buried in the lines of my callused palms
and thinking
"All this is a disease we share."

I sip a glass of mysterious wine
and then dance with you.
My body,
a withering flower,
opens,
murmuring
"Take it!
Take everything in this world!
Clean like death."

III. Dawn

With their old money
men bet on the fresh lips
of young girls.
The world is no longer new.

At 3 a.m.
thieves walk freely.
The man at the next table announces
"The restaurant is closed."

You jump up,
smash the radio,
the noisy music,
the glass surface,
our futile arguments.

I'm recalling
a shabby hotel in 1972
where I rouged my lips
under an old curtain embroidered with Chinese insects.

Soon we walk out of the gate.
Heaven is deeply asleep,
but I'm used to
walking into Hell.

I'm thinking
"The net of love has a wide mesh.
What can one see through old age?"
Love exhausted
floats like a ship on vacation.

Little by little we're aging.
Some friends
who live in remote towns
still call me by my first nickname.
As our car passes through Manhattan,
I remember
the old northwest country.

"Your place
or mine?"
you whisper
in the rain.

Proof

The last ray of dusk stabs me.
I lie on the naked land, to prove
that my blood is mixed with a river
and I'll never feel sad. Under me,
the sunset tans the white scattered rocks.
When I cross my hands, dark falls
and dreams ruin me immediately.
I am at a loss, trapped
by the drunken glare of twilight.

Water changes me; it describes
a lonely color. I can't settle down.
I'm a boundless woman.
The look in my eye turns to amber
to penetrate the mind and make it less accessible.
The heart's shadow
displays itself all night long on the rock, to prove
that the silence in the sky is beyond human power.

When I rise and turn into blue morning flames
autumn becomes colder—
Women, your sweetness
is last month's disaster
but today you're at peace, rising out of darkness
to give comfort.

End

What about when it's over? That day
I hoisted my baby into the air, and returned to
the original center, standing like a tree.
From the underground, blood spurted up and lifted me.
Now I open new eyes
to the sky: What about when it's over?

Look, don't turn your face away.
Seven days became a week to follow me.
Many satisfying dreams gather around me.
An unspeakable
pain starts and is inscribed
onto the sky: What about when it's over?

The echo is like a predictable road.
Current shoots into the fatal heel.
I no longer know: What about when it's over?
Another voice in the air, clear:
no doubt this is the last question.
Why does no one answer: What about when it's over?

I no longer care about my secret.
It becomes transparent like an October moan.
You must expect the end in silence.
Some psychic communication makes me stare into the dark.
All winter I've been asking with a smile,
who can tell me: What about when it's over?

中国蜂蜜

张耳

延绵不绝的故事，发生过的
和将要发生的
过去，小心拂动触角，手滑
没有折点，东方妇人的肌肤
水蛇出没，曲线游移，洞穴
游戏，音符，文字，游戏，无声的
歌流向脚趾，龃龉的失去，裹纹骨髓
冰河隐伏，热盘裸露
大红床单紧裹不确定的情绪，伸缩如箕
赞诵者漂然踱步，腰部柔软
潺流地呻吟

延绵不绝的时钟敲
从一个点到另一个点，思维
不连续的轨迹，没有缓冲
星象，掌纹，激光透视，心理治疗，识别
面目全非，你无言以对
歌一行行漂去
世纪剑的缠绕仍缠绵不清
藤蔓，发丝，流水，蔓藤
山的高矮陡然迷蒙
破碎的报顶伸说铜锈斑驳的
手指警醒地亲吻花器，异域
风延绵不绝

中国蜂蜜

Zhang Er was born in Beijing. Her poems have appeared and are forthcoming in American Letters, Commentary, China Press, and First Line. She is the translator into Chinese of, among others, John Ashbery and Denise Levertov. She is the author of *Winter Garden*, a collection of poems from Goats and Compass Press. A medical doctor and research scientist, she lives in Manhattan.

Raindrop

It's not difficult to go against thewind—
   just overcome the resistance.
It's not difficult to go with the wind either—
   merely obey inertia.

   A raindrop
   suspended in space
   winds back and forth
   the winds come from six directions.

Winds come from six directions.
The fractured bones of an umbrella
become a flag—
stark banner of the rain.

ZHANG ER

Chinese Honey

Endless stories
   happened will happen
the past carefully shifting its antennae,
a caressing hand unaware of limits,
   a beautiful oriental skin.
Female, the snake merges and emerges
   in a wandering arc; from a cave
   come notes, plays on words.
Soundless song
lapping at the toes, a pointed
indigo tongue, the suddenness of chill.
Icy river—hidden—exposed warm lips:
   scarlet bed sheets,
uncertainty, sweeping back
   and forth like flag.
The dream walker strolls indifferently,
   flexible of waist, exaggerated of moan.

Endless drum beats
   from beat to beat
thought on a discontinuous track
   without cognition:

Line by line the song drifts,
twiners of the last century still twining,
   wisteria, long hair, running springs.

202

The heights of a mountain lost in the haze,
        the spoken peak vigilantly extends
            its rusty fingers,
kissing the flower dew, the exotic land
Endless wind.

Chinese honey.

来呀，天神
这些人又在闹了
且趁我飞离之机
我不知道为何泪水流满
为何撕破了揉纸为何
躲进衣柜寻求黑暗的庇护

我低低地却用尽全力呐喊
我觉得喉咙在流血而词语无力
天花板上面有老鼠在乱蹿
电灯摇晃着象钟摆一下一下无情
我恍然大悟：
我那诚卸掉的耻辱正是我
那应有的责任
我已不配有这敌人
没有人召唤我
我只是一个自作多情的小鸡仔
将随便遇到的庞然大物当生母
这一切真好笑

Zhang Zhen was born
in Shanghai in 1962.
She withdrew from
Fudan University in
Shanghai and emi-
grated to Sweden
where she studied
film-making. She
returned to Beijing
in 1985, participating
in poetry readings,
journal publishing
and art exhibitions,
until 1988, when she
moved to Japan for
three years, where
she received a BA in
literature. She is
presently a graduate
student in
comparative literature
at the University of
Iowa. Zhang Zhen
has been writing
poetry since 1980.
Her work has
appeared in *Today*,
and she has three
mimeograph
collections of poetry.

Poetry

Poetry is a kind of weather.
A light flashes from dark clouds.
A cosmic ray
bombards your roof
and lights your candles,

a kind of thunder,
heavy, distant,
that doesn't pour down rain but spills milk.
Because of this you'll never grow old.
Expectations are conquered.

The blood you shed to test the knife
is her way
of showing us the sources of things.
Your life
is in her leather pocket.

She's the beauty you accept in pain,
the thirst of people who live in the sun.
At the end, a storm will come.
Rest in peace.
She'll send you a wreath.

Revolution

Come, gods!
These people are fighting again.
I'm flying away.
I don't know why I'm crying,
why I'm tearing up the newspaper,
or hiding in the closet.

I shout, softly, with all my strength.
My throat is bleeding but my words are powerless.
Mice scuttle above the ceiling,
the lamp swings like a clock's pendulum.
It suddenly dawns on me that
I am the humiliation and the responsibility
I've tried to avoid.
I don't deserve an enemy.
No one calls for me,
I'm only a sentimental chick
who takes a giant she met by accident for her mother.
What a farce—
Let me laugh till my belly hurts, till I faint.

Revolution no longer has anything to do with me.
With no place to splatter my hot blood,
I pour it into an ice bucket.
It's excellent for making cocktails.

"But you're wrong again," says one of the gods,
placing his hand on my heart,
his face against my hair.
"Little woman, you are a revolution."
I watch fire engines sweep by every day,
but no one can put out the fire.

I'll carry the luggage of freedom
and travel around the world to stir up trouble.
When summer comes,
when it's my birthday,
the gods will visit me,
and we'll dance into the dawn.

Zhao Qiong, who
is of Manchu
nationality, was born
in Shanxi Province in
1959. She studied
English at Qiqihar
Teachers' College and
has translated
*Selected Poems of the
Confessional School,
Selected Poems of the
Beat Generation,* and
T.S. Eliot's play
*Murder in the
Cathedral.* She is a
poet and painter.
Her book, *Collected
Poetry and Paintings
of Zhao Qiong,* is
forthcoming from
the Hong Kong
International
Expectation Press.
She is the editor of
Art World at the
Shanxi Arts Institute.

Hidden Arc

A bullet pierces the orchestral score.
Cicadas cha-cha loudly in my jewelry box.

Sap drips
through the eye
of a needle.

I examine my conscience: thoughts
like red bats transcend moral waves.
I look but I don't see.
I swallow everything I possess.
Suspicion is a fox, circling madly.
Nightmares are prowling wolves.

Out of the grave a pair of white butterflies
glides under the rainbow.
The cool drizzle
feeds the sun in the east....

ZHAO QIONG

Doubt

It's been years
since the crow made a confession behind the house.
The old tree is gone.
The girl who used to enjoy the shade
has become someone else's wife.

An empty envelope crosses the rainy season
like a stuffed swallow
on a dark cloud.

Who can stop the minute hand from meeting the hour hand?
Not all midnight points to twelve.
At the last stroke
the moon throws a tantrum inside the glass clock.

Now I take out my golden horn
and place it in alcohol and flame.
The crystal bottle is full of oxygen.
Flowers bloom at a moment's notice.

Evening comes, along with the philosopher's wrinkles.
My anxious lover has
one foot on the ladder,
the other stuck in cement.

Punctual Arrival

Memory tosses
and paces.
You step on your own shadow
while the sunshine stretches into an endless day.

The philosophical concrete collapses,
exposing thin iron bars.
Women take deep breaths
and curse madly.

On the illuminated sea floor
double-tailed fish bump against the fence.
The stone bank sinks.
Someone screams from the womb.
The charging eyes
shut tight in fire.
Did you hear a faint moan?

You who are about to set off
for the world,
please delay your journey.

郑单衣诗选

致秋天　　　郑单衣

垮就垮吧，秋天
没有谁可以动摇我

我的镰刀
悬在心头
没有谁可以使它不生锈

它明晃晃
有着更冷的意志
它带着我
渡过山银的河

渡过山银的河
它带着我
在发高烧的树林里徘徊

佝偻的正义象鱼刺
我卡在鱼刺上
举着我的镰刀倒退
我和整个秋天一起倒退

我望久了醉醺醺的鱼
总是醉醺醺的
我望久了秋天的部队和风
在塔尖上

我望久呐，再望久……
云是那更高的眺望者

不死。不死就是广汪的沉默
就是改造、洗头、高音喇叭
……
就是……
就是啊就是……

对于秋天，我只有愤怒、石头和铁
对于你，我只有纸和失眠

Zhen Danyi was born in Zigong, Sichuan, and spent his childhood in the countryside with his maternal grandmother. At eighteen, he began studying chemistry at Southwest Teachers' College, and was the editor of the journals *College Students' Poetry* and *Modern Chinese Poetry*. After graduation in 1985, he was assigned to the Guizhou Agriculture Institute, where he still teaches. Since 1981, his poems have appeared in *Shanghai Literature, Poetry Journal,* and *First Line.* His mimeograph books include *Thirty-three Poems* (1986), *Seventeen Poems* (1987), *Sixteen Poems* (1988), *Poems: 1989,* and *Poems: 1990.* A collection of his work called *Pomegranate* is forthcoming.

To Autumn

If you want to collapse, Autumn, go ahead.
Nothing can shake me.

My harvest sickle
hangs on the wall of my heart.
Nothing can keep it from rusting.

Gleaming
with cold
it takes me
across the mercury river.

But first
I must wander
in a feverish forest.

Diminished justice is like a fishbone.
I'm pierced to the marrow,
reeling back with my sickle
and the end of autumn.

I see the fish
eternally drunk.
I see autumn's army,
the wind
on a pagoda roof.

Zhen Danyi

Still alive. But to live means silence,
reform, washing my hair, broadcasting, etc.

Means...
means and means...

For autumn, I have anger, stone, and iron.
For you, I have only paper and insomnia.

Poem

I give it all to you, April and May's bleeding gold, July's
evil wheel, the electrified sky and an extinguished
torch, to you,
a sword, a cryptic metaphor, a spilled
bottle, and all my remaining property, all to you.

Gems, poison, splintered hell, to you,
even if it were heaven or a paper moon,
I'd give it all to you, even if
it were another pretense, another betrayal, even if
it were an umbrella which couldn't be closed,
    squandered money,

even if it were a garden stone disguised as jade, a rotten fish
climbing stairs, even if
it were a bag of potatoes, buried deep in life,
even if it were a boat of mud at sea, a plague, a shower,
the moaning of a wrecked train—

there's more I want to give you—
a broken house, a reluctant autumn,
an impatient springtime paralyzed like a flaccid
    whip, a meaningless
word or expired prescriptions. I want to give you

a complete act, a dull knife, an unforgettable
pain, and here's something else—
this smashed clock, my heart, crying, go for
it, it's my last heaven, take it,
this ruin, this inferno, it's all yours!

割 麦 人

邹静之

割麦人
他的镰刀磨得飞快
他的酒也像镰刀

那些麦子等着倒下
像一些远之的朋友
走过来倒进怀里

他听到
麦子接触刀的声音
他是刀
他也是麦子

假如没有冬天
割麦人会放弃收获
酒在割他喉咙时
他总这样想

A native of Beijing,
Zou Jingzhi has
been publishing
poetry since the
early eighties in the
journals *Poetry,
October, Harvest,*
and *First Line.* His
book *Streamer* came
out in 1989,
published by Culture
and Art Press. He
also writes plays and
screenplays, and edits
Poetry magazine.
He lives with his
family in Beijing.

The Meridian Gate

Arriving on horseback the descendants of old China
open their hands to shoot at the five high towers.

They turn to the square
and the heavy shadow of the monuments.
They pass the ninety-nine stone blocks.
In front of the Meridian Gate
covered with ninety-nine iron nails
they listen to the executions.
Outside the red gate
They see the blood
splashing the walls.

Others crawl among the weeds that grow here every year,
their knees kicking up dust. The heavy imperial carriages
crush their bodies, those lands of skin and flesh.
Their semen and blood smear history.
They have already died thousands of times.
Savage weapons
cut short the cries of the beheaded.
Their eyes fix on the animal handles of the wide open gate.
They stare hard at today

The Wheat Reaper

The wheat reaper
has ground his sickle
sharp.
His wine is ripe too,
ready as the sickle.

The wheat is waiting
to fall
like friends from far away
who come over
to collapse into your arms.

He can hear
the sound of sickle meeting wheat.
He is that sickle.
He is that wheat.

If there were no winter
the reaper would give up harvesting.
Wine soothes
as it stings his throat.

ZOU JINGZHI

To Die in a Sitting Position

At the sound of your voice
those who are gone or going away
stand still.
Different images float in the air, ascending to heaven.
A tawny finger
plucks the string of a distant memory.
You walk away to lie in the sunny marsh.
From a different angle the May sun makes love to you.

You loiter on the street corner
watching the world piece itself together then fall apart.
When you start moving,
every life stops to look.
When you think of women,
you knit your brows or smile openly.
The flag on the tower is playing with the wind.
It makes you think of her body surging like a wave,
the same body that sheared the city
of its sex.

You reach out your hand
and penetrate her skin like a hero.
You think of the snow that covered the fields all winter
and the fresh damp air.
Someday
you will no longer belong to yourself or to anyone else.
You will become a wriggling sprout out of the ancient past.
That moment only takes a second on your watch.
Within that second your life ends then begins again.

Death is the destination of birth.
This Buddhist eulogy is depressing.
On another day in another situation
you thought about many women and their seducing postures
by drawing inferences
about other cases
from one instance.

You predicted the destinations of all journeys.
That short second is a complete life.
Day is day,
night is night.
You and the women are all rusty machines.
You close your eyes vertiginously.
You embrace to keep warm
and wait for the next samsara,
while thoughts ferment discreetly
between transmigrations.
You no longer restrain yourself from fantasizing
about other women when you make love.
One night you suddenly see through your own face.
Waking up the next morning you say
to the only star in the sky:
                "I wish I could die quickly
                so I could be born again."

Burning the Red Soil

Hejimuya yuoya loyayaya ya

—the speaker at the fire

Holding the torch of five thousand years,
we enter the history books.
We start at the end and go backwards,
dynasty by dynasty, till we reach a blank page.
We burn a line of words—

Five thousand years of civilization.

It is said that mother and father
fell in love because of water, and reproduced by fire
as red as menstrual blood—land resting
after a harvest.
At a glance, five thousand years
are as short as the moment when a baby sucks milk.

Fire comes out of wood and burns metal.
Because of the fire
this thin red wall
hardens into pottery,
then into bronze,
and the sound of the yellow bell
of fire and gold
echoes through history,
every character sonorous
and bright—

Five thousand years of civilization.

From *Yellow Tiles and Red Walls*

The Well of Imperial Concubine Zhen

The gate of hell, so gloomy and cold,
so deep and far away,
opens and closes at the bottom of the dry well.
Girls dare not bend to look in,
afraid of a hand pushing them from behind.

Concubine Zhen died thin.
Widowed for many years,
the dowager feared the laughter between man and woman,
feared that Zhen's graceful steps and her perfume
would blind the eye of the emperor.

She ordered Zhen to die
and the emperor to love another.

Crying, Zhen said she didn't want to die or pollute the well.
If she died the emperor would also perish....
Before she finished speaking, she was pushed
into a long distant night.

She's been floating ever since.

What's in My Heart

There's a bird calling at night,
a little bird
calling from the gloomy tree in the cold.
It's the same bird I've seen
in a tree on the plain
calling me.

I'm not a bird.
I can't fly.
I'm not a little bird.
I can't call back.
But my eyes can
turn into stars
hanging from a twig,
and accompany the bird till twilight.

There's a bird under my eyes,
a sleeping bird.
Its cries, one after another, have sunk
into the farthest place of my heart.

Zou Jingzhi

Old Bowl

Old bowl, older than me,
feeds our family.
Ordinary blue patterns, pottery rough
as a valley.

Old bowl enters life like
a mother, silently
holds clean food, those
fruits of labor
given to us from her bosom. Old bowl
keeps our family together.

Everyone washes her with water
to make her shine with clean solid light
like a peasant woman walking in the fields.

Old bowl has no damage, no damage.
She survives fire and flood.
But she's old
and is used only at special events
to hold ordinary food.

The Translators

Elizabeth Fox is the author of *Limousine Kids on the Ground,* a collection of prose poems and essays. Her work has appeared in many magazines and anthologies.

Ed Friedman is the artistic director of The Poetry Project at St. Mark's in the Bowery. He has written nine individual or collaborative books, the most recent being *Mao & Matisse.*

Lyn Hejinian is co-editor of *Poetics Journal.* Her recent books include *The Cold of Poetry, Oxata,* and *My Life.*

S.J. King is is a poet and the author of many scholarly articles. He lives in the New York metropolitan area.

Gary Lenhart's newest poetry collection is *Father and Son Night.* He edited *The Teachers & Writers Guide to William Carlos Williams.* Lenhart teaches at Dartmouth College.

Dick Lourie is a poet, musician and a co-editor of Hanging Loose Press. His most recent collection is *Ghost Radio* and his CD of poems with blues band is forthcoming.

Murat Nemet-Nejat is a poet and essayist. He wrote *The Bridge,* a book-length poem, and he has translated two books from the Turkish, *I, Orhan Veli* and *A Blind Cat Black & Orthodoxies* by Ece Ayhan.

Ron Padgett is the author of many books, including *New & Selected Poems* and *The Big Something.* He translated *The Complete Poems of Blaise Cendrars.* Padgett is publications director of Teachers & Writers Collaborative and teaches at Columbia University.

David Shapiro is the author of many books, including *After a Lost Original, To an Idea* and *Lateness.* He teaches art history at William Patterson College and has won fellowships from the National Endowment for the Arts and the National Endowment for the Humanities.

Leonard Schwartz is the author of *Words Before the Articulate*, a poetry collection, and co-editor of *New Poets of the Nineties*. His translations of Chinese poetry have appeared in *Journal of Chinese Religions, Poetry New York*, and other journals.

Richard Sieburth's latest book of translation is *Selected Writings of Gérard de Nerval*. He has also translated works by Blanchot, Benjamin, and Hölderlin.

Jeff Twitchell-Waas presently lives in Singapore. A collection of his translations of Che Qianzi's work, *Original: Chinese Language-Poetry Group*, was published in 1994.

Anne Waldman is director and co-founder of the Jack Kerouac School of Disembodied Poets at the Naropa Institute.

Keith Waldrop is co-founder of Burning Deck Press and teaches at Brown University. His book, *The Silhouette of the Bridge*, won the America Award in Poetry.

Wang Ping was born in Shanghai and graduated from Beijing University in 1984. She moved to the United States the following year and recently earned her doctorate from New York University. She has published three books: *American Visa* (stories); *Foreign Devil* (novel); and *Of Flesh and Spirit* (poetry) and won fellowships from the National Endowment for the Arts and the New York Foundation for the Arts.

Lewis Warsh's many books include such poetry collections as *Avenue of Escape* and *Private Agenda*, and two novels, *A Free Man* and *Agnes & Sally*. He is editor and publisher of United Artists Books and teaches at Long Island University.

Zhen Zheng holds degrees from Nanjing University and the University of Alabama. She now lives in Hong Kong.

Made in the USA
Columbia, SC
28 July 2020